Vocabulary Skills, G

Contents

Introduction 2

Vocabulary List 3

Overall Assessment 1 4

Overall Assessment 2 6

Unit 1: In the Past

Assessment 8

Lesson 1
Priscilla and the Queen 10

Lesson 2
The Warning 13

Lesson 3
The Great Wall of China 16

Lesson 4
In Times of War 19

Lesson 5
The Stonecutter and the King 22

Unit 2: School

Assessment 25

Lesson 6
The Play 27

Lesson 7
Dear Nan 30

Lesson 8
The Decision 33

Lesson 9
First Day of School 36

Lesson 10
A School Discussion 39

Unit 3: Pets

Assessment 42

Lesson 11
Baxter 44

Lesson 12
The Wolves 47

Lesson 13
Polar Bears of the Arctic 50

Lesson 14
Deep in the Ocean 53

Lesson 15
Zeus 56

Unit 4: Careers

Assessment 59

Lesson 16
Architects 61

Lesson 17
Photojournalism 64

Lesson 18
Computer Graphics 67

Lesson 19
Rescue Pilot 70

Lesson 20
Archeologist 73

Unit 5: Word Analysis

Assessment 76

Lesson 21
Prefixes 78

Lesson 22
Suffixes 81

Lesson 23
Latin Roots 84

Lesson 24
Homophones 87

Lesson 25
Cultural Words 90

Fun with Context Clues 93

Fun with Homophone Riddles 94

Answer Key 95

Vocabulary Skills, Grade 6, Introduction

One of the most basic elements of reading comprehension is understanding the meaning of words. However, students may not realize that they do not necessarily need to know the meaning of every word in a selection in order to understand what they are reading. They may be surprised to find that through reading, they can actually increase their knowledge of word meaning. The more words students know, the more they will be able to read, and conversely, the more they read, the more words they will know.

Students can use several strategies to help them determine the meaning of unfamiliar words they encounter while reading:
• using context clues
• analyzing prefixes, suffixes, and root words
• looking up unfamiliar words in the dictionary

Vocabulary Skills is designed to help students practice these strategies in order to incorporate them seamlessly into their approach to reading. New vocabulary words are introduced within the context of high-interest readings. Students can use these context clues to determine the meaning of unfamiliar words. Activities are designed to reinforce the use of all word-meaning strategies.

By increasing their word power, students will also increase their scores on standardized tests.

Organization
The book is organized into five units, with five lessons in each unit. In Units 1–4, each lesson consists of a high-interest reading rich in context so that students can determine the meaning of the vocabulary words based on the context of the reading. Each lesson includes vocabulary activities and most contain a dictionary activity. The vocabulary activities include
• analogies,
• antonyms,
• base words,
• classifying,
• compound words,
• crossword puzzles,
• multiple meanings,
• synonyms,
• word groups,
• word puzzles, and
• word webs.

The dictionary skills include
• alphabetical order,
• guide words,
• syllabication, and
• pronunciation.

Each lesson provides a review of the vocabulary words, once again in a context-based approach, and gives students the chance to practice using the vocabulary words in their own original writing.

Unit 5 focuses on word analysis, with lessons dealing specifically with prefixes, suffixes, Greek and Latin roots, homophones, and words from other languages. The book concludes with a fun section so that students have the opportunity to play games with words.

Assessments
Vocabulary Skills uses two kinds of assessments:
• Two overall assessments located at the front of the book cover all the new vocabulary words. One of these can be given as a pretest to gauge students' knowledge of the vocabulary. Later in the year, the other test can be administered to determine students' understanding, progress, and achievement.
• Each unit also has an assessment. These unit assessments can be administered at any time during the unit as a pretest, review, or posttest.

Vocabulary List
On page 3 is a list of all the vocabulary words contained in Units 1–4. You may want to distribute it to students so they will be able to incorporate the words into their writing for other assignments.

Correlation to Standards
The National Council of Teachers of English has stated in the "Standards for the English Language Arts" the following: "Students apply a wide range of strategies to comprehend, interpret, evaluate, and appreciate texts. They draw on their prior experience, their interaction with other readers and writers, their knowledge of word meaning and of other texts, their word identification strategies, and their understanding of textual features (e.g., sound-letter correspondence, sentence structure, context, graphics)." *Vocabulary Skills* helps students achieve this goal by providing strategies for students to comprehend what they read, increase their knowledge of word meaning, and expand their use of context clues.

Dictionaries and Other Reference Books
Students striving to increase their vocabulary benefit greatly from having access to dictionaries, thesauruses, and other books dealing with word meanings and origins. These resources should be readily available to students at all times.

Vocabulary List

abominable (7)
adorned (5)
aggressive (12)
animosity (7)
antics (11)
applauded (10)
appointed (1)
aristocrat (10)
aspect (10)
assessed (15)
assignment (8)
assurances (15)
avid (17)

background (6)
barrier (3)
belligerently (4)
bestowed (2)
binoculars (13)
bizarre (9)
boisterously (11)
bonds (1)
breathtaking (6)
bulky (12)

caressed (11)
caribou (13)
carnivorous (13)
casually (9)
clamor (2)
classroom (6)
coincidences (15)
commended (15)
competitions (15)
complex (9)
condescendingly (7)
consideration (16)
consist (16)
consult (16)
conversed (1)
conviction (8)
courtiers (1)
crevice (20)

critically (19)
debris (20)
despondently (7)
determination (8)
devoted (1)
disarm (7)
discarded (11)
disdainfully (4)
dispatch (18)
distinctive (12)
diversity (14)
dominated (10)
dress rehearsal (6)
dubious (20)

efficient (16)
elective (8)
embarked (3)
emphasized (10)
encountered (14)
enthusiastically (11)
equilibrium (18)
ethnic (10)
exasperated (4)
excavation (20)
exhaustion (2)
expeditions (17)

faint (14)
feat (2)
flawlessly (15)
flusters (9)
footage (18)
frantic (19)
frustration (4)
function (16)
futile (5)

glimpse (19)

harsh (3)
haughty (12)
hibernation (13)
high-spirited (6)

hostile (5)
humility (5)
implication (7)
implored (2)
indicate (19)
informal (10)
intervals (3)
intimidating (12)
invaders (3)

kennels (11)

landscape (17)
league (4)
legendary (17)
loudspeaker (6)
luminous (14)

magnitude (7)
manipulate (18)
marathon (2)
massive (20)
mend (12)
mesmerized (1)
migration (13)
minute (14)
mischievously (15)
mispronounced (9)
mission (19)
monumental (17)

nomadic (3)

occupation (4)
ominously (20)
options (8)

panel (10)
perplexed (8)
persuade (5)
plundering (20)
potential (14)
precisely (1)
predator (13)
prey (13)

priority (3)
procedure (18)
procrastinated (8)
profile (17)

ration (4)
recalls (9)
recommend (8)
relics (20)
remote (12)
residents (16)
retrieve (12)
reverting (7)
revived (5)
rugged (17)

sarcastically (9)
scorned (15)
self-confident (6)
significant (5)
simulate (18)
snuggled (11)
sophisticated (9)
spontaneous (17)
stadium (2)
stage fright (6)
storage (16)
striving (1)
structure (16)
submersible (14)
summon (5)
superimposed (18)
swerved (2)

temples (19)
transmission (19)
tundra (13)
turbulent (19)

unwavering (4)

vast (3)
versatile (18)

waves (14)
whimpered (11)

Note: The numbers in parentheses refer to the lessons where the vocabulary words are taught.

Name _____ Date _____

Overall Assessment 1

Darken the letter of the word that fits best in the sentence.

1. The beautiful view from the top of the mountain was _____.
   - Ⓐ boring
   - Ⓑ haughty
   - Ⓒ breathtaking
   - Ⓓ avid

2. Jason said some _____ things to Kyle that hurt his feelings.
   - Ⓐ courtiers
   - Ⓑ abominable
   - Ⓒ caressed
   - Ⓓ bulky

3. "I don't think I'll ever hit the baseball," said Kayla _____.
   - Ⓐ enthusiastically
   - Ⓑ cheerfully
   - Ⓒ despondently
   - Ⓓ mischievously

4. Students were asked to share an _____ food that represented the country they researched.
   - Ⓐ ethnic
   - Ⓑ magnitude
   - Ⓒ nomadic
   - Ⓓ versatile

5. The two bears growled at each other to show their _____.
   - Ⓐ implication
   - Ⓑ hibernation
   - Ⓒ bonds
   - Ⓓ animosity

6. The restaurant had several food _____ to choose from for lunch.
   - Ⓐ waves
   - Ⓑ temples
   - Ⓒ intervals
   - Ⓓ options

7. Rita did not get her reading assignment done because she _____ until the last minute.
   - Ⓐ procrastinated
   - Ⓑ bestowed
   - Ⓒ adorned
   - Ⓓ perplexed

8. Ask the waitress to _____ a desert that she thinks is really good.
   - Ⓐ maneuvered
   - Ⓑ demonstrated
   - Ⓒ inquired
   - Ⓓ recommend

9. Grandpa _____ stories about the time he lived on a farm.
   - Ⓐ recalls
   - Ⓑ antics
   - Ⓒ waves
   - Ⓓ dubious

10. The crowd cheered and _____ when the play was done.
    - Ⓐ emphasized
    - Ⓑ applauded
    - Ⓒ embarked
    - Ⓓ snuggled

11. Ricardo invited his friends to a small, _____ gathering to watch the football game.
    - Ⓐ ration
    - Ⓑ tundra
    - Ⓒ informal
    - Ⓓ unfurled

12. Talk of the upcoming school dance _____ the conversation.
    - Ⓐ implored
    - Ⓑ swerved
    - Ⓒ dominated
    - Ⓓ whimpered

Overall Assessment 1, page 2

Darken the letter of the word that means the same, or about the same, as the boldfaced word.

13. a **devoted** friend
- Ⓐ loyal
- Ⓑ missing
- Ⓒ useless
- Ⓓ positive

14. **appointed** to the committee
- Ⓐ reported
- Ⓑ researched
- Ⓒ selected
- Ⓓ shown

15. **implored** the mayor
- Ⓐ helped
- Ⓑ stopped
- Ⓒ begged
- Ⓓ told

16. **embarked** on a trip
- Ⓐ halted
- Ⓑ started
- Ⓒ planned
- Ⓓ joined

17. went around a **barrier**
- Ⓐ world
- Ⓑ tree
- Ⓒ person
- Ⓓ obstacle

18. **harsh** weather conditions
- Ⓐ unpleasant
- Ⓑ beautiful
- Ⓒ cooler
- Ⓓ stormy

Darken the letter of the correct answer.

19. Which word comes from the Latin root *man*, which means "hand"?
- Ⓐ America
- Ⓑ manual
- Ⓒ mane
- Ⓓ demand

20. Choose the homophone that correctly completes the sentence.
Tia took a walk in the fresh _____.
- Ⓐ ere
- Ⓑ heir
- Ⓒ air
- Ⓓ hair

21. Which word is a noun and a verb?
- Ⓐ antics
- Ⓑ landscape
- Ⓒ avid
- Ⓓ disarm

22. Choose the word that gives the meaning of the underlined prefix.
Jan had to <u>re</u>write the article.
- Ⓐ again
- Ⓑ always
- Ⓒ not
- Ⓓ with

23. Which suffix can be added to the root word *sorrow* to make a new word?
- Ⓐ ful
- Ⓑ ly
- Ⓒ est
- Ⓓ ous

24. Which word is an adjective?
- Ⓐ office
- Ⓑ talking
- Ⓒ beautiful
- Ⓓ quickly

Overall Assessment 2

Darken the letter of the word that fits best in the sentence.

1. Elliot went to _____ with his teacher about his science project.
   - Ⓐ mend
   - Ⓑ consult
   - Ⓒ submersible
   - Ⓓ indicate

2. The _____ in the apartment building wanted the hallways painted.
   - Ⓐ courtiers
   - Ⓑ binoculars
   - Ⓒ residents
   - Ⓓ invaders

3. Mr. Edwards did not have room for all of the furniture, so he put some in _____.
   - Ⓐ storage
   - Ⓑ conviction
   - Ⓒ crevice
   - Ⓓ invaders

4. Lola was an _____ skier and spent many hours skiing down the mountain.
   - Ⓐ caribou
   - Ⓑ avid
   - Ⓒ bizarre
   - Ⓓ conversed

5. Ron painted a _____ picture of the lake in the springtime.
   - Ⓐ revived
   - Ⓑ simulate
   - Ⓒ profile
   - Ⓓ landscape

6. Mrs. Oliver was a famous mountain climber who led _____ to the snowy peak.
   - Ⓐ antics
   - Ⓑ carnivorous
   - Ⓒ expeditions
   - Ⓓ debris

7. The doctor told Alex that removing stitches was a _____ that could be done in the office.
   - Ⓐ procedure
   - Ⓑ panel
   - Ⓒ occupation
   - Ⓓ transmission

8. The _____ wind caused the plane to shake.
   - Ⓐ spontaneous
   - Ⓑ background
   - Ⓒ nomadic
   - Ⓓ turbulent

9. Pat planned to do a science fair project that would _____ a volcano.
   - Ⓐ migration
   - Ⓑ elective
   - Ⓒ simulate
   - Ⓓ humility

10. Quan caught a _____ of a deer before it ran into the woods.
    - Ⓐ vast
    - Ⓑ glimpse
    - Ⓒ futile
    - Ⓓ feat

11. Ella was on a _____ to discover which store had the best-priced videos.
    - Ⓐ doorway
    - Ⓑ partition
    - Ⓒ mission
    - Ⓓ voyage

12. Rachel had to push hard to open the _____ wooden door.
    - Ⓐ massive
    - Ⓑ minute
    - Ⓒ plundering
    - Ⓓ dubious

Overall Assessment 2, page 2

Darken the letter of the word that means the same, or about the same, as the boldfaced word.

13. played **boisterously**
- (A) sadly
- (B) wonderfully
- (C) loudly
- (D) quietly

14. whimpered softly
- (A) talked
- (B) wiped
- (C) laughed
- (D) cried

15. retrieve the bucket
- (A) get back
- (B) give to
- (C) buy
- (D) fill

16. the **luminous** fish
- (A) glowing
- (B) hungry
- (C) long
- (D) scaly

17. performed **flawlessly**
- (A) helpfully
- (B) happily
- (C) horribly
- (D) perfectly

18. build a **structure**
- (A) well
- (B) playground
- (C) building
- (D) garden

Choose the letter of the correct answer.

19. Which prefix can be added to the root word *behave* to make a new word?
- (A) mis
- (B) un
- (C) dis
- (D) im

20. Choose the homophone that correctly completes the sentence.
Which _____ of shoes did you buy?
- (A) pare
- (B) pair
- (C) pear
- (D) peer

21. Which suffix makes *nation* mean "relating to a nation"?
- (A) able
- (B) y
- (C) ous
- (D) al

22. Choose the root word of *unforgettable*.
- (A) for
- (B) table
- (C) get
- (D) forget

23. Which word is a verb?
- (A) hostile
- (B) bulky
- (C) options
- (D) dispatched

24. Which word is both a verb and an adjective?
- (A) vast
- (B) aristocrat
- (C) faint
- (D) casually

Unit 1 Assessment

Darken the letter of the word that fits best in the sentence.

1. The _____ wore their finest silk clothes when they attended the court.
   - Ⓐ accountants
   - Ⓑ courtiers
   - Ⓒ servants
   - Ⓓ bonds

2. The two women _____ in the park while the children played.
   - Ⓐ conversed
   - Ⓑ maneuvered
   - Ⓒ devoted
   - Ⓓ attended

3. The banker was _____ by the mayor to a finance committee.
   - Ⓐ searched
   - Ⓑ determined
   - Ⓒ forced
   - Ⓓ appointed

4. Maria leaves for school at _____ seven o'clock each day.
   - Ⓐ precisely
   - Ⓑ sometimes
   - Ⓒ eagerly
   - Ⓓ outrageously

5. The children, _____ by the puppet play, sat and watched without moving.
   - Ⓐ uninterested
   - Ⓑ bored
   - Ⓒ mesmerized
   - Ⓓ noticed

6. A _____ is a race that is 26 miles long.
   - Ⓐ course
   - Ⓑ target
   - Ⓒ sprint
   - Ⓓ marathon

7. The tired and hot football players sat down in _____ when the game was over.
   - Ⓐ exhaustion
   - Ⓑ exhilaration
   - Ⓒ anticipation
   - Ⓓ communication

8. Mark _____ his parents to let him go with his friends to a rock concert.
   - Ⓐ demanded
   - Ⓑ implored
   - Ⓒ avoided
   - Ⓓ startled

9. The _____ was filled with loyal sports fans to watch the big game.
   - Ⓐ sidewalk
   - Ⓑ court
   - Ⓒ stadium
   - Ⓓ station

10. Ryan could hear the _____ of the fire truck as it raced down the street.
    - Ⓐ vegetation
    - Ⓑ clamor
    - Ⓒ feat
    - Ⓓ victory

11. The principal _____ a medal of honor upon the scout troop for their work in the community.
    - Ⓐ removed
    - Ⓑ hoarded
    - Ⓒ designed
    - Ⓓ bestowed

12. Mr. Pollard _____ on a journey this morning that would take him to five different countries.
    - Ⓐ inhabited
    - Ⓑ congregated
    - Ⓒ embarked
    - Ⓓ recounted

Unit 1 Assessment, page 2

Darken the letter of the word that fits best in the sentence.

13. Many _____ tribes use horses to help them carry their belongings when they move.
    Ⓐ approaching
    Ⓑ enemy
    Ⓒ original
    Ⓓ nomadic

14. When the tree fell across the road, it became a _____ that was difficult to go around.
    Ⓐ barrier
    Ⓑ gateway
    Ⓒ statue
    Ⓓ project

15. States in the Midwest are known for their _____, cold winters.
    Ⓐ mild
    Ⓑ tropical
    Ⓒ harsh
    Ⓓ isolated

16. The _____ yelled noisily as they broke down the castle doors.
    Ⓐ invaders
    Ⓑ magicians
    Ⓒ jugglers
    Ⓓ emperors

17. The citizens' daily lives became unbearable during the _____ of the victorious army.
    Ⓐ enemy
    Ⓑ occasion
    Ⓒ tribe
    Ⓓ occupation

18. The boys held their dogs apart, but the animals continued to bark _____ at each other.
    Ⓐ successfully
    Ⓑ foolishly
    Ⓒ belligerently
    Ⓓ graciously

19. Which soccer _____ did Dana join?
    Ⓐ player
    Ⓑ league
    Ⓒ concert
    Ⓓ summit

20. Paul felt a high level of _____ when he could not reach the next level on his computer game.
    Ⓐ frustration
    Ⓑ relief
    Ⓒ accomplishment
    Ⓓ organization

21. The students tried to _____ their teacher to let them enjoy a night without homework.
    Ⓐ congregate
    Ⓑ increase
    Ⓒ command
    Ⓓ persuade

22. Mrs. Thomas sent a student to _____ Mark to her office.
    Ⓐ inhabit
    Ⓑ summon
    Ⓒ advance
    Ⓓ refuse

23. Many diamonds _____ the singer's dress.
    Ⓐ adorned
    Ⓑ hampered
    Ⓒ concealed
    Ⓓ splintered

24. The other team had so many points that Greta thought it was _____ to continue the game.
    Ⓐ remarkable
    Ⓑ expected
    Ⓒ revived
    Ⓓ futile

Name _____ Date _____

Priscilla and the Queen

Read the story. Think about the meanings of the words in bold type.

Priscilla had been one of the **courtiers** of the queen's court. She attended all the special events with the other dukes, duchesses, and important people in England. Priscilla was **mesmerized** by the quiet and gracious queen. She would stand in line to greet the queen and watch every move the royal woman made. The queen had noticed Priscilla too, and **conversed** with the young girl on several occasions. Priscilla was honored when the queen had **appointed** her to be a lady-in-waiting.

Priscilla was entirely **devoted** to the queen. She spent mornings, afternoons, and evenings **striving** to please the queen in every way. She carried out the queen's requests **precisely** and performed her duties perfectly. Priscilla's devotion to the queen especially showed in her caring manner. Over the years, special **bonds** of trust and friendship developed between the two women.

Look back at the words in bold type. Use clues in the story to figure out the meaning of each word. Write each word on the line next to its meaning.

_____ **1.** loyal and faithful

_____ **2.** putting forth a strong effort

_____ **3.** people who go to the royal court

_____ **4.** talked with

_____ **5.** feelings that hold people together

_____ **6.** hypnotized

_____ **7.** selected for a duty or job

_____ **8.** exactly; accurately

Base Words

Base words are words without any endings or other word parts added to them. Some endings are
s, ed, ing, and ly. Sometimes the spelling of the base word changes when an ending is added to it.

EXAMPLES:

step	steps	open	opened
drive	driving	glad	gladly

Write the base word of each word below. Then, use the base word in a sentence.

1. striving _____

_____

2. devoted _____

_____

3. bonds _____

_____

4. courtiers _____

_____

5. precisely _____

_____

6. appointed _____

_____

7. mesmerized _____

_____

8. conversed _____

_____

Dictionary Skills

A **verb (v.)** is a word that shows action. However, actions may not show movement.
Some verbs are linking verbs and tell what something <u>is</u> or <u>was</u>.
EXAMPLE: The queen **excused** her ladies-in-waiting.
The queen **was walking** in the garden.

Look at the vocabulary words above. Write the five words that are verbs.

_____

_____

Word Wise

| devoted | appointed | courtiers | bonds |
| striving | conversed | precisely | mesmerized |

Choose the word from the box that makes sense in the sentences below.

1. The _____ were invited to the royal palace by the queen.

2. Parents feel strong _____ with their children.

3. The baby stared at the bird, _____ by its ability to talk.

4. Mr. Edwards comes home each day at _____ six o'clock.

5. Alex sold lemonade all summer because he was _____ to raise money for a sports camp.

6. The principal _____ Sam to lower the school flag each day.

7. The dog was _____ to its master and followed each command.

8. Mrs. Alton _____ with the neighbors who walked by her house.

Writing

Write your own story about what it would be like to have served a queen long ago. Use as many of the vocabulary words from the box as you can.

_____

_____

_____

_____

_____

_____

_____

_____

_____

Name _____ Date _____

The Warning

Read the story. Think about the meanings of the words in bold type.

Warships! Why had they come during the Olympic Games, a time of peace? Penelope had to warn the king!

Quickly, she ran toward Athens. She followed the **marathon** course, the longest race in the Olympic Games. She **swerved** to avoid runners as she passed them. After nearly two hours, Penelope was near **exhaustion**. Her side hurt and she could only breathe in shallow pants, but the **clamor** of the excited crowds in the distance told her she was close to her destination. At last, Penelope stumbled onto the **stadium** track and across the finish line. She **implored** the startled onlookers to help her warn the king.

For her courage and strength, the grateful king **bestowed** upon her the laurel crown of victory given to Olympic champions. "Your **feat** will never be forgotten," he said, "and surely your name will live in history."

Look back at the words in bold type. Use clues in the story to figure out the meaning of each word. Write each word on the line next to its meaning.

_____ **1.** presented to

_____ **2.** turned aside from one's course

_____ **3.** begged; pleaded with

_____ **4.** loud and continuous noise

_____ **5.** an act that shows great courage or skill

_____ **6.** a place where many people sit and watch sports

_____ **7.** a long, running race of 26 miles

_____ **8.** the state of being tired

Analogies

An **analogy** shows how two words go together in the same way as two other words.
EXAMPLE:
Glass is to break as paper is to tear.

Think about how the words in the first pair go together. Write the word from the box to complete the analogy.

feat	stadium	implored	marathon
clamor	swerved	bestowed	exhaustion

1. Quiet is to solitude as loud is to _____.

2. Accept is to reject as commanded is to _____.

3. Hair is to hare as feet is to _____.

4. Short is to sprint as long is to _____.

5. Skate is to rink as football is to _____.

6. Exhilaration is to excited as _____ is to tired.

7. Given is to gift as _____ is to award.

8. Paddled is to saddled as _____ is to curved.

Dictionary Skills

A **noun (n.)** is a word that names a person, place, thing, or quality.
EXAMPLE: The **runners** crossed the finish **line**.

Look at the vocabulary words in the box above. Write five words that are nouns.

_____

_____

_____

_____

Word Wise

feat	stadium	implored	marathon
clamor	swerved	bestowed	exhaustion

Rewrite each sentence. Use one of the words from the box in place of a word or phrase in the sentence. Make any changes necessary.

1. Sara turned aside from her course to avoid hitting the cat on the sidewalk.

_____

2. The football fans stood and cheered as the players ran into the place to play sports.

_____

3. People from around the world came to run the 26-mile race.

_____

4. The mayor presented a medal to the police officer who had saved the child trapped by a flooded river.

_____

5. Mrs. Kendall begged her son to be careful during the game because he had just gotten a cast off his arm.

_____

6. Muriel felt that skiing down the steep hill was quite a big act of courage.

_____

7. Nancy was near being very tired after playing two softball games in a row.

_____

8. The loud noise of the audience encouraged the actors to take another bow.

_____

Writing

Write your own story about a time you got an award. Use as many of the vocabulary words from the box as you can.

_____

_____

_____

The Great Wall of China

Read the letter. Think about the meanings of the words in bold type.

Dear General Li:

I am glad to hear that you have **embarked** on the wall-building project. I am sure you will agree that we must protect ourselves from the approaching enemies. In fact, our enemies have grown stronger because they have joined forces with **nomadic** tribes that camp along our borders. Our top **priority**, then, is to create a sturdy **barrier**. This obstacle should have lookout towers at regular **intervals** so guards can watch for the opposing armies.

I know you are concerned about beginning the project in the winter, especially since the **harsh** weather will slow down **invaders** anyway. Still, I insist there is no time to waste. Our empire is **vast**. I have vowed to protect its wide-ranging border once and for all.

Sincerely,

Emperor Qin

Look back at the words in bold type. Use clues in the letter to figure out the meaning of each word. Write each word on the line next to its meaning.

_____ **1.** wandering, roaming

_____ **2.** rough or unpleasant

_____ **3.** distances between objects or points

_____ **4.** begun; set forth

_____ **5.** very wide and extensive

_____ **6.** something that ranks of high importance

_____ **7.** people who attack

_____ **8.** something that blocks the way

Synonyms

A **synonym** is a word that has the same, or almost the same, meaning as another word.
EXAMPLES: small—little   like—enjoy   busy—active

Write the letter of the synonym beside each word.

_____ **1.** barrier   **A.** roaming

_____ **2.** embarked   **B.** importance

_____ **3.** invaders   **C.** obstacle

_____ **4.** harsh   **D.** begun

_____ **5.** nomadic   **E.** unpleasant

_____ **6.** intervals   **F.** extensive

_____ **7.** priority   **G.** spaces

_____ **8.** vast   **H.** attackers

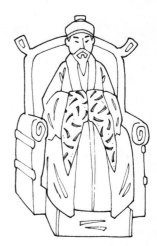

Dictionary Skills

A dictionary can help you find out how to say, or pronounce, a word. A dictionary has a **pronunciation key** that lists the symbols for each sound. It also gives a familiar word in which the sound is heard. A pronunciation key usually appears on every other page of the dictionary.

a	add	i	it	o͞o	took	oi	oil
ā	ace	ī	ice	o͞o	pool	ou	pout
â	care	o	odd	u	up	ng	ring
ä	palm	ō	open	û	burn	th	thin
e	end	ô	order	yo͞o	fuse	th̶	this
ē	equal					zh	vision

ə = { a in *above*   e in *sicken*   i in *possible*
       o in *melon*   u in *circus* }

Example: guitar (gi tärʹ)

Use the pronunciation key to help you say the vocabulary words in parentheses ( ) in the sentences below. Write the regular spelling for each word in ( ).

1. The police officers stood at (inʹ tər vəlz) along the parade route. _____

2. The (nō madʹ ik) people often live in tents. _____

3. The park covers a (vast) area. _____

4. It is Tom's top (prī orʹ ə tē) to complete his project before the weekend. _____

Word Wise

vast	priority	nomadic	embarked
harsh	barrier	invaders	intervals

Choose the word from the box that makes sense in the sentences below.

1. John _____ on a tour of the United States that will last two months.

2. The ocean was a _____ area of blue.

3. The fence was a _____ that the dog could not jump.

4. Mrs. Ramos made it a _____ to greet each parent at the meeting.

5. Some tribes lead a _____ life and follow a herd of animals.

6. Water stations were set up at _____ along the race course.

7. The _____ moved quickly across the land, attacking anyone who tried to stop them.

8. People who climb high into the mountains find the land to be very _____ and cold.

Writing

Imagine that you are General Li. Write your own letter in response to the emperor. Use as many of the vocabulary words from the box as you can.

_____

_____

_____

_____

_____

_____

_____

_____

_____

_____

In Times of War

Read the story. Think about the meanings of the words in bold type.

During wartime, soldiers are not the only people who must act with **unwavering** courage. For example, ordinary citizens might have to respond with dignity when enemy soldiers try to cause trouble by behaving **belligerently**. Although most people would feel **exasperated** by such bullying, it is both brave and wise to control one's anger. No matter how unworthy the behavior, acting or speaking **disdainfully** can only cause more trouble.

Another source of anger and **frustration** during wartime can be the search for scarce supplies. In America during World War II, some foods were so scarce that each person was given a **ration** of the item for a month. The situation in enemy-occupied countries was much worse than in the Unites States since the **occupation** army also had to be fed. Such conditions often resulted in people forming a **league** and attempting to overthrow the enemy.

Look back at the words in bold type. Use clues in the story to figure out the meaning of each word. Write each word on the line next to its meaning.

_____ **1.** a fixed amount, especially food

_____ **2.** not giving way or failing

_____ **3.** taking land by military force

_____ **4.** in a warlike manner

_____ **5.** irritated or annoyed

_____ **6.** in a way that looks down on someone or something

_____ **7.** a sense of not being satisfied

_____ **8.** a group of people joined together for a common purpose

Multiple Meanings

Some words have more than one meaning. You can use clues in the sentence to tell which meaning the word has.

EXAMPLE: produce

meaning A: to bring forth. We watched the magician **produce** a rabbit out of thin air!

meaning B: fresh fruit and vegetables. We bought **produce** at the market.

Write the letter of the correct meaning next to each sentence.

ration

meaning A: a fixed amount, especially food

meaning B: to give out in portions

_____ **1.** Grandma talks about the time during the war that she had to pick up the family's ration of sugar.

_____ **2.** The teacher will ration the snacks to the children.

league

meaning A: a group of people joined together for a common purpose

meaning B: a measure of distance

_____ **3.** A league is equal to about three miles.

_____ **4.** Who is your favorite team in the football league?

occupation

meaning A: taking land by military force

meaning B: the work a person does

_____ **5.** The occupation of the town ended when the enemy soldiers were chased out.

_____ **6.** Mike thought repairing cars would be an interesting occupation.

Word Wise

ration	occupation	unwavering	disdainfully
league	frustration	exasperated	belligerently

Choose the word from the box that makes sense in the sentences below.

1. Mrs. Rubins was _____ that her son had not cleaned his room.

2. The dog stayed by its master's bed with

_____ loyalty.

3. The candidate running for office spoke

_____ about his opponent.

4. Sugar was an important _____ during World War II.

5. Mr. Thomas invited an artist to tell about her _____ and the skills needed to do it.

6. The champion team in each baseball _____ plays in the world series.

7. The lady was very angry and yelled _____ at the surprised sales clerk.

8. The toddler cried in _____ when it could not reach the shiny toy.

Writing

Imagine that you live in a town occupied by enemy soldiers. Write your own story about conditions in the town. Use as many of the vocabulary words from the box as you can.

_____

_____

_____

_____

_____

_____

Name _____   Date _____

The Stonecutter and the King

Read the story. Think about the meanings of the words in bold type.

The king's advisers tried to **persuade** him to increase the size of his army, but their efforts were **futile**. "I have defeated every **hostile** army that has ever tried to attack my empire," he said. "My power is well known. "No," he went on, "I have more **significant** concerns." Sharply, he ordered a servant to **summon** the best artist in the kingdom.

A simple stonecutter was brought into his presence. The stonecutter bowed to the king in **humility**.

"This palace is far too plain to reflect my own greatness," said the king. "I want the outer walls **adorned** with carvings of a thousand life-size horses and soldiers. You have one month to complete them."

The stonecutter was so shocked by the king's order that he fainted and had to be **revived** by the king's own doctor.

Look back at the words in bold type. Use clues in the story to figure out the meaning of each word. Write each word on the line next to its meaning.

_____ **1.** decorated; added to the beauty of

_____ **2.** useless; having no effect

_____ **3.** feeling or showing anger

_____ **4.** the quality of being without pride

_____ **5.** brought back to life or consciousness

_____ **6.** to order to come

_____ **7.** to cause to do or believe by giving reasons

_____ **8.** having special value or meaning

Name _____ Date _____

Antonyms

Antonyms are words with opposite meanings.
EXAMPLES: loud—soft   fast—slow   hard—easy

Match the words in the box with their antonyms listed below. Write the words on the lines.

futile	summon	adorned	significant
hostile	revived	persuade	humility

_____ **1.** effective

_____ **2.** stripped

_____ **3.** peaceful

_____ **4.** unimportant

_____ **5.** dispatch

_____ **6.** killed

_____ **7.** pride

Dictionary Skills

An **adjective (adj.)** describes a noun. Most adjectives tell what kind, which one, or
how many.
EXAMPLE: The **young** stonecutter used the **metal** tools to chisel the **large** stone.

Look at the vocabulary words above. Write the three words that are adjectives.

_____

_____

_____

Word Wise

futile	summon	adorned	significant
hostile	revived	persuade	humility

Rewrite each sentence. Use one of the words from the box in place of a word or phrase in the sentence. Make any changes necessary.

1. Sara's ring was decorated with diamonds and pearls.

_____

2. The clue the detective found was very important in helping to solve the mystery.

_____

_____

3. Brian apologized to his father with no pride when he found out that his father had been right all along.

_____

_____

4. Before I face the crowd of reporters, I must call forth all my courage.

_____

5. The dog barked in an angry manner when the cat ran into its yard.

_____

6. Once the ship ran aground and wrecked, it was useless to save it.

_____

7. The photographer tried to talk Susan into posing for a picture.

_____

8. When Mrs. Kings fainted in the store, the manager brought her back to consciousness.

_____

Writing

Write your own story telling about a time you were asked to do an impossible task. Use as many of the vocabulary words from the box as you can. Use another sheet of paper.

Unit 2 Assessment

Darken the letter of the word that means the same, or about the same, as the boldfaced word.

1. high-spirited children
- Ⓐ sad
- Ⓑ lively
- Ⓒ helpful
- Ⓓ slow

2. a **breathtaking** view
- Ⓐ dirty
- Ⓑ distant
- Ⓒ small
- Ⓓ exciting

3. of great **magnitude**
- Ⓐ large size
- Ⓑ need
- Ⓒ heaviness
- Ⓓ happiness

4. answered **despondently**
- Ⓐ angrily
- Ⓑ hopelessly
- Ⓒ eagerly
- Ⓓ quickly

5. reverting to bad behavior
- Ⓐ thinking about
- Ⓑ talking about
- Ⓒ going back to
- Ⓓ leaving behind

6. showed **animosity**
- Ⓐ anger
- Ⓑ friendliness
- Ⓒ excitement
- Ⓓ horror

7. see **abominable** actions
- Ⓐ awful
- Ⓑ funny
- Ⓒ exhausting
- Ⓓ interesting

8. think about different **options**
- Ⓐ colors
- Ⓑ foods
- Ⓒ choices
- Ⓓ magazines

9. procrastinated on their homework
- Ⓐ tried
- Ⓑ remembered
- Ⓒ forgot
- Ⓓ waited

10. an interesting **assignment**
- Ⓐ picture
- Ⓑ book
- Ⓒ task
- Ⓓ store

11. feeling **perplexed**
- Ⓐ puzzled
- Ⓑ sick
- Ⓒ useless
- Ⓓ superior

12. to **recommend** a movie
- Ⓐ see
- Ⓑ buy
- Ⓒ find
- Ⓓ suggest

13. had the **conviction**
- Ⓐ story
- Ⓑ product
- Ⓒ belief
- Ⓓ fun

14. studied with **determination**
- Ⓐ friends
- Ⓑ firmness
- Ⓒ help
- Ⓓ materials

Unit 2 Assessment, page 2

Darken the letter of the word that means the same, or about the same, as the boldfaced word.

15. a **bizarre** event
- Ⓐ loud
- Ⓑ unusual
- Ⓒ silly
- Ⓓ wonderful

16. recalls a story
- Ⓐ reads
- Ⓑ tells
- Ⓒ forgets
- Ⓓ remembers

17. a **complex** problem
- Ⓐ simple
- Ⓑ different
- Ⓒ difficult
- Ⓓ dangerous

18. spoke **sarcastically**
- Ⓐ sharply
- Ⓑ softly
- Ⓒ calmly
- Ⓓ gently

19. mispronounced a word
- Ⓐ looked up
- Ⓑ said out loud
- Ⓒ said correctly
- Ⓓ said incorrectly

20. flusters easily
- Ⓐ embarrasses
- Ⓑ yells
- Ⓒ cleans
- Ⓓ stretches

21. a **panel** of parents
- Ⓐ group
- Ⓑ choice
- Ⓒ crowd
- Ⓓ sample

22. dominated the game
- Ⓐ organized
- Ⓑ played
- Ⓒ lost
- Ⓓ controlled

23. emphasized a word
- Ⓐ stressed
- Ⓑ wrote
- Ⓒ added
- Ⓓ deleted

24. the audience **applauded**
- Ⓐ booed
- Ⓑ clapped
- Ⓒ left
- Ⓓ shouted

25. an **informal** party
- Ⓐ large
- Ⓑ small
- Ⓒ casual
- Ⓓ surprise

26. ethnic traditions
- Ⓐ popular
- Ⓑ cultural
- Ⓒ social
- Ⓓ ancient

27. had **stage fright**
- Ⓐ scared to act on stage
- Ⓑ scared to see a play
- Ⓒ scared to wear csotumes
- Ⓓ a scary part of a play

28. acted **sophisticated**
- Ⓐ jealous
- Ⓑ childish
- Ⓒ worldly
- Ⓓ guilty

The Play

Read the story. Think about the meanings of the words in bold type.

The students in Mr. Carlos' class put on a play titled "The Fools of Chelm and the Stupid Carp." It was a **high-spirited** play that the students approached with great enthusiasm. While most practices took place in the **classroom**, the **dress rehearsal** took place on the stage. It was the first time that the students saw all the different parts of the play all at once, including the **background** scenery and the costumes. All together, it was **breathtaking**!

On the night of the performance, all the students were nervous, but the lead actor, Jim, developed a bad case of **stage fright**. Then, Mr. Carlos spoke to Jim and assured him that the nervousness would pass. When Jim heard the opening music on the **loudspeaker**, he seemed to calm instantly. Jim walked on stage with a **self-confident** air. No one in the audience ever suspected that the play almost did not go on.

Look back at the words in bold type. Use clues in the story to figure out the meaning of each word. Write each word on the line next to its meaning.

_____ **1.** a room in which classes are held

_____ **2.** a system that makes sounds louder

_____ **3.** a belief in one's abilities and worth

_____ **4.** lots of energy; very lively

_____ **5.** a play practice with all costumes and props before the first performance

_____ **6.** exciting; thrilling

_____ **7.** the part of a scene that is in the distance

_____ **8.** a feeling of being scared when performing in front of people

Name _____ Date _____

Compound Words

A **compound word** is a word formed by putting two or more words together. The meaning of the word is related to the meaning of each individual word. Compound words may be written as one word, as hyphenated words, or as two separate words.

EXAMPLES: sunrise, high-rise, orange juice

Join one word from Column A with one from Column B to make a compound word. Write the new words. Add a hyphen if needed. Use each word one time.

Column A	Column B	
dress	confident	1. _____
self	room	2. _____
breath	fright	3. _____
high	rehearsal	4. _____
back	speaker	5. _____
stage	spirited	6. _____
class	taking	7. _____
loud	ground	8. _____

Dictionary Skills

An **adjective (adj.)** describes a noun. Most adjectives tell what kind, which one, or how many.

EXAMPLE: The **beautiful** actress wore a **blue** gown covered with **many** rhinestones.

Look at the compound words you wrote above. Write the three words that are adjectives.

_____

_____

_____

Name _____   Date _____

Word Wise

classroom	background	high-spirited	breathtaking
loudspeaker	stage fright	self-confident	dress rehearsal

Rewrite each sentence. Use one of the words from the box in place of a word or phrase in the sentence. Make any changes necessary.

1. Lana thought the view from the mountaintop was thrilling.

_____

2. The students walked into the place of learning when they heard the bell.

_____

3. After winning the award, Kira was more believing in her abilities.

_____

4. Each morning, the principal makes the announcements on the system that makes sounds louder.

_____

5. Mrs. Jenkins thought her students were too full of energy, so she took them to the gym to play basketball.

_____

6. The musician got scared before going on stage and did not want to play.

_____

7. Fred found that he needed a chair on stage when the people did a practice of the play.

_____

8. Keesha is part of the stage crew that paints the scene in the distance.

_____

Writing

Write your own story about a play experience. Use as many of the vocabulary words from the box as you can.

_____

_____

_____

Dear Nan

Read the advice column. Think about the meanings of the words in bold type.

Dear Nan Sanders,

There's a girl I like in school. I try to talk with her, but she only smiles **condescendingly**, as if I'm not worth her attention. I think another boy has been saying **abominable** things about me to her. Would it help if I told her a few bad things I know about him?

Unhappy in Akron

Dear Unhappy,

Living up to your name by thinking **despondently** and acting depressed will do you no good. What's more, **reverting** to childish behavior by becoming a tattletale may be seen as an **implication** of immaturity. Hide your **animosity** for the other boy by acting in a pleasant manner. By doing this, you will both **disarm** him and impress her. And cheer up! While this affair of the heart has great **magnitude** now, it probably will seem less important in a few months. Good luck!

Look back at the words in bold type. Use clues in the advice column to figure out the meaning of each word. Write each word on the line next to its meaning.

_____ **1.** suggestion

_____ **2.** hateful; disgusting

_____ **3.** going back to

_____ **4.** great size or extent

_____ **5.** to make harmless

_____ **6.** feelings of anger

_____ **7.** hopelessly

_____ **8.** in a superior manner

A Crossword Puzzle

Use the clues and the words in the box to complete the crossword puzzle.

disarm	abominable	implication	condescendingly
reverting	animosity	magnitude	despondently

Across

1. to make harmless
6. having an air of being better than others
8. feelings of anger

Down

2. going back to
3. hateful or disgusting
4. great size or extent
5. hopelessly
7. suggestion

Word Wise

disarm	abominable	implication	condescendingly
reverting	animosity	magnitude	despondently

Choose the word from the box that makes sense in the sentences below.

1. After appearing on a commercial on television, Rachel acted _____ to all of her friends.

2. You can often _____ someone who makes a nasty comment with just a smile.

3. A calm smile is a clear _____ that you are in control.

4. During the argument, the students began calling each other names and _____ to other childish behavior.

5. Doug began acting _____ after his best friend left for a summer camp.

6. When Pam offered to lead the group, she did not realize the _____ of the project.

7. The people running for office said _____ things about each other on their television ads.

8. The two dogs growled at each other to show their _____.

Writing

Think about a problem you have seen at school. Write a letter to Nan about the problem. Then, trade papers with a classmate. Pretend to be Nan and write an answer. Use as many of the vocabulary words from the box as you can in each letter.

_____

_____

_____

_____

_____

_____

The Decision

Read the story. Think about the meanings of the words in bold type.

Enrico sat with Mrs. Baines, the school counselor. He was trying to decide what courses to take for the next school year. Mrs. Baines explained each course and suggested several **options** that Enrico should take. She knew that Enrico was an ambitious student. He wanted to go to college someday. Enrico never **procrastinated** on any of his schoolwork, and he did each **assignment** immediately and carefully. Moreover, his good grades showed the **determination** with which he studied. But Enrico was still **perplexed** as to which language **elective** to sign up for.

"I **recommend** that you take Italian," said Mrs. Baines. "You already speak Spanish, and the two languages are similar."

Enrico agreed. He had the **conviction** that he would do well in the Italian language course. Enrico filled out the form and thanked Mrs. Baines for her suggestion.

Look back at the words in bold type. Use clues in the story to figure out the meaning of each word. Write each word on the line next to its meaning.

_____ **1.** an optional course

_____ **2.** will power

_____ **3.** to speak in favor of

_____ **4.** a task that is given

_____ **5.** confused

_____ **6.** put off doing something

_____ **7.** a strong belief

_____ **8.** things that may be chosen

Synonyms

A **synonym** is a word that has the same, or almost the same, meaning as another word.
EXAMPLES: cheerful—happy   instructed—taught

Choose the word from the box that matches its synonym. Write the word on the line.

options	perplexed	recommend	assignment
elective	determination	conviction	procrastinated

1. belief _____

2. puzzled _____

3. optional course _____

4. waited _____

5. choices _____

6. suggest _____

7. task _____

8. firmness _____

Dictionary Skills

A **verb (v.)** is a word that shows action. However, actions may not show movement. Some verbs are linking verbs and tell what something <u>is</u> or <u>was</u>.
EXAMPLES: Enrico **was** happy.
Enrico **walked** home.

Look at the vocabulary words above. Write the three words that are verbs.

_____

_____

Word Wise

options	perplexed	recommend	assignment
elective	determination	conviction	procrastinated

Choose the word from the box that makes sense in the sentences below.

1. "I _____ that you should do your homework before we go," said Mother.

2. Rita did not know which ice cream to order because there were too many _____.

3. Greg chose art as his school _____.

4. The students groaned when they heard the teacher's homework _____.

5. The mountain climber began climbing the mountain with great _____.

6. Our teacher held the _____ that students learned best when they participated in the lesson.

7. Sam _____ until the last minute to do his math homework.

8. Mei-Ling asked the teacher how to say a word that _____ her.

Writing

Write your own story about a time someone helped you make a decision. Use as many of the vocabulary words from the box as you can.

_____

_____

_____

_____

_____

_____

_____

_____

_____

Name _____ Date _____

First Day of School

Read the story. Think about the meanings of the words in bold type.

Most students have at least one story to tell about a **bizarre** or funny event that happened on the first day of school. Brett tells about the time he strolled **casually** down the hall, trying to look cool and **sophisticated**. He did not realize that one of his baby sister's pink socks was stuck to the back of his jacket. Tonya **recalls** the time she took a diagnostic test for math. She correctly answered all the **complex** problems, but she missed several simple ones. Maya is shy and **flusters** easily, and she remembers having to correct every teacher who **mispronounced** her name. Sal remembers the gym teacher who asked her **sarcastically** if she had ever swung a bat before. Instead of answering angrily, Sal smiled and kindly answered "yes." Then, she proved it by hitting a run on the next pitch.

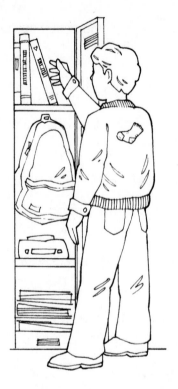

Look back at the words in bold type. Use clues in the story to figure out the meaning of each word. Write each word on the line next to its meaning.

_____ **1.** said a word the wrong way

_____ **2.** done without thought or planning

_____ **3.** becomes nervous or embarrassed

_____ **4.** hard to understand

_____ **5.** strange; unusual

_____ **6.** showing much knowledge and experience

_____ **7.** remembers

_____ **8.** spoken in a sharp manner that is hurtful

Antonyms

Antonyms are words with opposite meanings.
EXAMPLES: loud—soft   fast—slow   hard—easy

Match the words in the box with their antonyms listed below. Write the words on the lines.

recalls	casually	complex	sophisticated
bizarre	flusters	sarcastically	mispronounced

_____ **1.** simple

_____ **2.** naive

_____ **3.** pronounced

_____ **4.** usual

_____ **5.** forgets

_____ **6.** kindly

_____ **7.** formally

_____ **8.** calms

Dictionary Skills

An **adverb** (**adv.**) is a word that tells more about a verb. It can tell about how, when, where, and how often an action takes place.

EXAMPLE: Suddenly, the dog ran **quickly** across the street. It was strange because he **never** runs over **there**.

Look at the vocabulary words above. Write the two words that are adverbs. Use each in a sentence.

_____

_____

Word Wise

recalls	casually	complex	sophisticated
bizarre	flusters	sarcastically	mispronounced

Choose the word from the box that makes sense in the sentences below.

1. Teachers have always _____ my name the first time we meet.

2. Lynn thought the new neighbors were very worldly and _____ when she saw they ate on real china.

3. Mark bought a _____ puzzle that had over one thousand pieces.

4. Missy would never answer a question _____ because she did not want to hurt her brother's feelings.

5. Grandpa _____ stories about the times when he was a young boy.

6. It _____ Sonya when she has to give a presentation in front of people.

7. All the guests were _____ sitting around the table and talking.

8. Erin made a _____ dress using different colors of tape.

Writing

Write your own story about something interesting that happened one year on the first day of school. Use as many of the vocabulary words from the box as you can.

_____

_____

_____

_____

_____

_____

_____

A School Discussion

Read the story. Think about the meanings of the words in bold type.

A **panel** of students from Latin America and
Vietnam discussed each **aspect** of life in their new
country. Since most people were interested in
school and social life, talk about these two areas
dominated the discussion. Juanita said that she
had made good friends in the United States, but
she **emphasized** that she still missed her old
friends in Mexico. Students wearing jeans and
T-shirts **applauded** when she observed that school
dress codes were much more **informal** here than
in Mexico. Kim pointed out that in Taiwan it was
easier to spot an **aristocrat** or a wealthy person,
because of his or her fine clothing. All the
students on the panel agreed that they liked living
in this country. However, most planned to carry on
at least some of their **ethnic** traditions as a link
with the countries they left.

**Look back at the words in bold type. Use clues in the story to figure out the meaning of each word.
Write each word on the line next to its meaning.**

_____ **1.** clapped to show enjoyment

_____ **2.** given special attention or stress

_____ **3.** a way that something can be looked at or
thought about

_____ **4.** not formal; casual

_____ **5.** having to do with a group of people who have the same
language and culture

_____ **6.** controlled because of importance

_____ **7.** a group

_____ **8.** a person who belongs to a high social position

Name _____   Date _____

Word Web

Fill in the word web with words from the box.

panel	informal	dominated	emphasized
ethnic	aspect	aristocrat	applauded

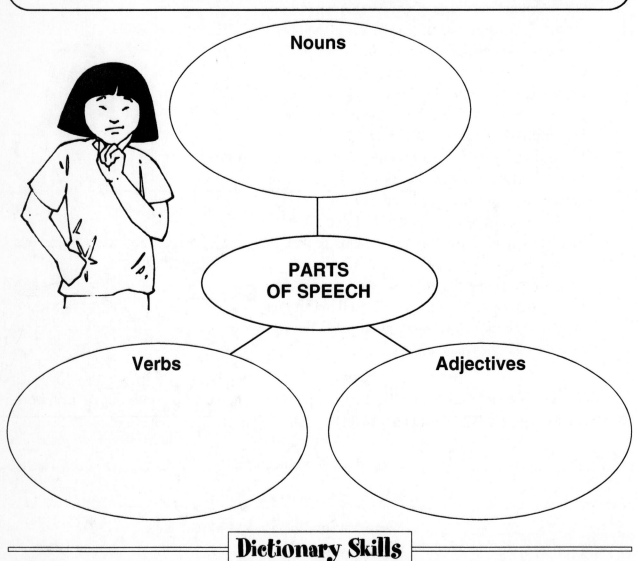

Nouns

PARTS OF SPEECH

Verbs

Adjectives

Dictionary Skills

Guide words are at the top of each page in a dictionary. Guide words tell the first and last entry words listed on the page. Every word listed on the page comes between the guide words.

Example: **treasure**   **tropical**   tremendous, trestle, trio, troll

Darken the circle for the correct answer.

1. Which word would be between the guide words *arrow* and *assign*?
   Ⓐ arrive   Ⓑ applaud   Ⓒ assemble   Ⓓ aristocrat

2. Which word would be between the guide words *embarrass* and *essay*?
   Ⓐ ethnic   Ⓑ easier   Ⓒ emphasize   Ⓓ embark

Word Wise

panel	informal	dominated	emphasized
ethnic	aspect	aristocrat	applauded

Choose the word from the box that makes sense in the sentences below.

1. The principal thought about every _____ of the problem before making a decision.

2. The students _____ when the presentation was over.

3. Mary told her friends they could wear jeans since the party was going to be _____.

4. Lord Byron was an _____ in England who wrote poetry many years ago.

5. Some parents were asked to be on a _____ to discuss ways to improve the parking lot traffic flow.

6. Talk of the best CD _____ the students' conversation.

7. People from many different _____ groups live in a large city.

8. The park ranger _____ that all dogs should be kept on a leash when they were in the park.

Writing

Write a paragraph telling why you like living in this country. Use as many of the vocabulary words from the box as you can.

_____

_____

_____

_____

_____

_____

_____

_____

Name _____ Date _____

Unit 3 Assessment

Darken the letter of the word that fits best in the sentence.

1. Paula visited several _____ when she decided to get a puppy.
   - Ⓐ marathons
   - Ⓑ stadiums
   - Ⓒ kennels
   - Ⓓ jewelers

2. The children roughhoused _____ in front of the television.
   - Ⓐ precisely
   - Ⓑ hungrily
   - Ⓒ seriously
   - Ⓓ boisterously

3. The children clapped and laughed at the _____ of the clown.
   - Ⓐ antics
   - Ⓑ exhaustion
   - Ⓒ creature
   - Ⓓ loneliness

4. "I'm ready to go to the pool!" shouted Mia _____.
   - Ⓐ enthusiastically
   - Ⓑ sorrowfully
   - Ⓒ angrily
   - Ⓓ guiltily

5. The puppy _____ quietly before falling asleep.
   - Ⓐ snoozed
   - Ⓑ whimpered
   - Ⓒ giggled
   - Ⓓ purred

6. After Dan opened the present, he _____ the box in the trash.
   - Ⓐ engaged
   - Ⓑ adorned
   - Ⓒ discarded
   - Ⓓ practiced

7. The mother _____ the cheek of her baby.
   - Ⓐ caressed
   - Ⓑ complicated
   - Ⓒ dribbled
   - Ⓓ speckled

8. Sue got a needle and thread so she could _____ a rip in her skirt.
   - Ⓐ shear
   - Ⓑ dye
   - Ⓒ tear
   - Ⓓ mend

9. The coach talked to his basketball team when he thought they were too _____ and pushy on the court.
   - Ⓐ polite
   - Ⓑ aggressive
   - Ⓒ eager
   - Ⓓ speedy

10. Tonya lives in a _____ part of the town where there are few houses.
   - Ⓐ busy
   - Ⓑ remote
   - Ⓒ populated
   - Ⓓ dated

11. Keisha put on a thick, _____ sweater that would keep her warm.
   - Ⓐ bulky
   - Ⓑ slight
   - Ⓒ transparent
   - Ⓓ complex

12. The ranger looked at the soaring eagle through the _____.
   - Ⓐ spectacles
   - Ⓑ mirror
   - Ⓒ binoculars
   - Ⓓ microscope

Unit 3 Assessment, page 2

Darken the letter of the word that fits best in the sentence.

13. Geese take turns flying in the lead during their _____.
- Ⓐ occasion
- Ⓑ imagination
- Ⓒ migration
- Ⓓ solution

14. Animals that eat meat are _____.
- Ⓐ porous
- Ⓑ herbivorous
- Ⓒ omnivorous
- Ⓓ carnivorous

15. The _____ is a cold region in the Arctic.
- Ⓐ tundra
- Ⓑ monsoon
- Ⓒ tropic
- Ⓓ rain forest

16. Diane tried to get a _____ splinter out of her thumb.
- Ⓐ minute
- Ⓑ tedious
- Ⓒ plastic
- Ⓓ curious

17. Margo feels that she has the _____ to be a famous dancer some day.
- Ⓐ patient
- Ⓑ possessive
- Ⓒ partition
- Ⓓ potential

18. Max saw a _____ light coming from a house down the road.
- Ⓐ blaring
- Ⓑ beam
- Ⓒ faint
- Ⓓ scheme

19. The two women hugged each other when they _____ each other at the store.
- Ⓐ encountered
- Ⓑ lectured
- Ⓒ distanced
- Ⓓ purchased

20. Tran was pleased at the _____ of courses offered by the school.
- Ⓐ dedication
- Ⓑ assorted
- Ⓒ sameness
- Ⓓ diversity

21. The moon looked like a _____ ball glowing in the sky.
- Ⓐ luminous
- Ⓑ frigid
- Ⓒ excessive
- Ⓓ irregular

22. The teacher _____ her students for their wonderful behavior on the field trip.
- Ⓐ ignored
- Ⓑ persisted
- Ⓒ commended
- Ⓓ resolved

23. The police officer _____ the damage that the burglar had done.
- Ⓐ assumed
- Ⓑ assessed
- Ⓒ excused
- Ⓓ reduced

24. The dog _____ its dinner and refused to eat.
- Ⓐ scorned
- Ⓑ snuggled
- Ⓒ gobbled
- Ⓓ shattered

Baxter

Read the story. Think about the meanings of the words in bold type.

Ben's parents finally agreed to let Ben get a dog. His father took him to visit several **kennels** and pet stores. Ben looked at all the dogs but couldn't find the perfect pet until he saw a small, spotted dog. When Ben put the puppy on the floor, it played **boisterously** around his feet. It jumped up on his jeans and nipped at his shoelaces. Ben and his dad laughed at the little dog's **antics**.

"This is the one!" Ben announced **enthusiastically**. "I'm naming him Baxter."

The clerk got a box and **discarded** the materials in it. Then, he put shredded paper in the bottom of a box. When Ben put the puppy in the box, it **whimpered** a little. Ben reached into the box and **caressed** the soft fur. Soon, the puppy **snuggled** down in the paper and went to sleep.

Look back at the words in bold type. Use clues in the story to figure out the meaning of each word. Write each word on the line next to its meaning.

_____ **1.** made a soft crying noise

_____ **2.** threw out something not wanted

_____ **3.** places where dogs are born

_____ **4.** laid close to

_____ **5.** showed affection; petted

_____ **6.** eagerly; excitedly

_____ **7.** in a noisy manner

_____ **8.** silly actions

Base Words

Base words are words without any endings or other word parts added to them. Some endings are **s**, **ed**, and **ly**. Sometimes the spelling of the base word changes when an ending is added to it.
EXAMPLES: step steps   open opened   glad gladly

Write the base word of each word below. Then, use the base word in a sentence.

1. kennels _____

_____

2. snuggled _____

_____

3. boisterously _____

_____

4. antics _____

_____

5. discarded _____

_____

6. whimpered _____

_____

7. enthusiastically _____

_____

8. caressed _____

_____

Dictionary Skills

An **adverb** (**adv.**) is a word that tells more about a verb. It can tell about how, when, where, and how often an action takes place.
EXAMPLE: Suddenly, the dog ran **quickly** across the street. It was strange because he **never** runs over **there**.

Look at the vocabulary words above. Write the two words that are adverbs.

_____

Name _____ Date _____

Word Wise

| antics | caressed | discarded | enthusiastically |
| kennels | snuggled | whimpered | boisterously |

Rewrite each sentence. Use one of the words from the box in place of a word or phrase in the sentence. Make any changes necessary.

1. The baby lay close in its mother's arms.

_____

2. Leo threw out the empty milk carton.

_____

3. The students shouted with eagerness and excitement on the last day of school.

_____

4. Cindy has a job after school feeding the animals at some places where dogs are born.

_____

5. Mrs. Quan laughed at the silly actions of her cat as it chased a ball of yarn.

_____

6. The baby cried softly before it went to sleep.

_____

7. Erin watched the monkeys climb noisily and with much action around their cage.

_____

8. Tia's cat always purred when she softly petted it.

_____

Writing

Write your own story about the antics of a puppy you have seen. Use as many of the vocabulary words from this lesson as you can.

_____
_____
_____
_____

The Wolves

Read the story. Think about the meanings of the words in bold type.

Karana stood back and looked at the fence. It had taken her all morning to **mend** it. Just as she bent down to **retrieve** the tools lying on the ground, she heard a **distinctive** howl. It could only mean one thing—the wolf pack was nearby. Karana spun around and scanned the horizon.

The wolves were gathered by the edge of the woods. The lead dog stood out in front. It was a **haughty** and proud animal. Karana could see its yellow eyes and **bulky** body. The huge size of it was very **intimidating**.

A shiver ran down Karana's back. The pack was getting much more **aggressive**. They usually didn't come out until late at night. But the wolf pack was one of the dangers of living in such a **remote**, unpopulated area. Karana hoped they would move on quickly. She had already lost several chickens. She did not want to lose more.

Look back at the words in bold type. Use clues in the story to figure out the meaning of each word. Write each word on the line next to its meaning.

_____ **1.** ready to attack

_____ **2.** far from cities or towns

_____ **3.** large size

_____ **4.** easy to recognize

_____ **5.** to repair

_____ **6.** frightening

_____ **7.** to get back

_____ **8.** very proud

Synonyms and Antonyms

Synonyms are words that have the same, or almost the same, meaning.
EXAMPLES: forested—wooded   humans—people   survive—live

Antonyms are words that have opposite meanings.
EXAMPLES: loss—gain   increasing—decreasing   never—always

Read each pair of words below. If the two words are synonyms, write _synonyms_. If the two words are antonyms, write _antonyms_.

1. intimidating—frightening _____

2. bulky—skinny _____

3. remote—populated _____

4. mend—break _____

5. haughty—proud _____

6. retrieve—discard _____

7. distinctive—common _____

8. aggressive—attacking _____

Dictionary Skills

An adjective (**adj.**) describes a noun. Most adjectives tell what kind, which one, or how many.
EXAMPLE: That frog sat on a **large** lily pad and ate **two** flies.

Look at the first word in each pair above. Write the six words that are adjectives.

_____

_____

_____

_____

_____

_____

Word Wise

mend	retrieve	haughty	intimidating
bulky	remote	aggressive	distinctive

Choose the word from the box that makes sense in the sentences below.

1. The _____ student thought he knew everything and would not accept help.

2. Flora bent down to _____ the book that was on the floor.

3. Mother had to _____ a rip in my shirt.

4. The campers pitched a tent in a _____ area where they would be alone.

5. I know when my father comes home because his car engine makes a

_____ squeak.

6. The dog growled and was very _____ when Marvin tried to take its bone.

7. Rhonda wore a big, _____ coat to stay warm.

8. Mr. Domingo's frown is very _____ and makes me shake in my shoes.

Writing

Write your own story about a time an animal scared you. Use as many of the vocabulary words from the box as you can.

_____

_____

_____

_____

_____

_____

_____

_____

_____

Polar Bears of the Arctic

Read the story. Think about the meanings of the words in bold type.

    Jorge was eager to continue his research. As he pointed his **binoculars** to the west, he spotted the polar bear in the distance. Its white fur was barely visible against the treeless landscape of the arctic **tundra**. The bear's winter sleep was finally over, and now that spring had come, the bear was awakening from its long **hibernation** to hunt for food.

    Jorge wondered what the animal's **prey** would be. Other bears eat both plants and animals, but a polar bear is mostly **carnivorous**. It eats fish, seals, and other arctic animals. In fact, a hungry bear is a dangerous **predator** even to large animals such as caribou. Jorge doubted, however, that the bear would find any **caribou** yet. The Arctic deer wouldn't make their **migration** north until later in the spring.

Look back at the words in bold type. Use clues in the story to figure out the meaning of each word. Write each word on the line next to its meaning.

_____ **1.** meat-eating

_____ **2.** an instrument for seeing long distances

_____ **3.** the movement from one geographical place to another

_____ **4.** the resting state that lasts through winter months

_____ **5.** an animal that is hunted for food

_____ **6.** deer native to the arctic region

_____ **7.** an animal that hunts for food

_____ **8.** the arctic plain

Word Puzzle

Write a vocabulary word next to each definition. Then, use the numbered letters to answer the question, "What animal can only be seen in the Arctic?"

1. an instrument for seeing long distances ____ ____ ____ ____ ____ ____ ____ ____ ____
 1

2. meat-eating ____ ____ ____ ____ ____ ____ ____ ____ ____ ____
 2

3. an animal that is hunted for food ____ ____ ____ ____
 3

4. the movement from one geographical place to another

____ ____ ____ ____ ____ ____ ____ ____ ____
 4

5. the resting state that lasts through winter months

____ ____ ____ ____ ____ ____ ____ ____ ____ ____
 5

6. an animal that hunts for food ____ ____ ____ ____ ____ ____ ____ ____
 6

7. the Arctic plain ____ ____ ____ ____ ____ ____
 7

Answer: ____ ____ ____ ____ ____ ____ ____
 1 2 3 4 5 6 7

Word Wise

prey	tundra	migration	hibernation
caribou	predator	binoculars	carnivorous

Use each vocabulary word in the box to write new sentences.

1. _____

2. _____

3. _____

4. _____

5. _____

6. _____

7. _____

8. _____

Writing

Research an animal that you think is interesting. Then, write a paragraph about that animal. Use as many of the vocabulary words from the box as you can.

_____

_____

_____

_____

_____

_____

_____

_____

_____

Deep in the Ocean

Read the letter. Think about the meanings of the words in bold type.

Dear Dad,

The deep ocean is largely unexplored and has a huge **potential** for numerous discoveries. Only a **minute** amount of information is known about the plants and animals that live there. Even when scientists use a **submersible**, they find it nearly impossible to travel deep enough.

The light from the sun does not reach to the depths of the ocean. It is pitch-black. However, scientists were surprised to find the **diversity** of sea life they **encountered**. They have discovered that some fish glow with a **faint** light that helps them attract prey. The black dragonfish is one such fish that is **luminous**. It **waves** its lighted feeler around its head hoping a smaller fish will swim nearby.

Look back at the words in bold type. Use clues in the letter to figure out the meaning of each word. Write each word on the line next to its meaning.

_____ **1.** a kind of submarine designed to dive into deep water

_____ **2.** something that can become possible

_____ **3.** a great variety or difference

_____ **4.** moves back and forth in a fluttering motion

_____ **5.** very small

_____ **6.** weak

_____ **7.** met unexpectedly

_____ **8.** glowing

Name _____ Date _____

Multiple Meanings

Some words have more than one meaning. You can use clues in the sentence to tell which meaning the word has.

EXAMPLE: fish

meaning A: a group of animals that live in water. We eat fresh **fish** at the beach.

meaning B: to pull out. I **fished** some coins out of my purse.

Write the letter of the correct meaning next to each sentence.

minute

meaning A: very small

meaning B: sixty seconds

_____ **1.** The quarterback scored a touchdown with less than a minute left in the game.

_____ **2.** Reba rubbed her eye to remove the minute speck of dirt.

faint

meaning A: weak

meaning B: to lose consciousness

_____ **3.** Chou heard the faint cry of a kitten coming from the bushes.

_____ **4.** John caught the woman just as she began to faint.

waves

meaning A: moves back and forth in a fluttering motion

meaning B: long ridges of water that move

_____ **5.** The child was scared of the big ocean waves.

_____ **6.** The girl on the parade float waves as she passes.

    Vocabulary Skills 6, SV 6905-1

Word Wise

waves	minute	potential	encountered
faint	diversity	luminous	submersible

Choose the word from the box that makes sense in the sentences below.

1. Larry looked out the window of the _____ and saw a fish with teeth.

2. There was a _____ chance that Darla would be able to join her friends at the movie.

3. We could see the _____ glow of the moon through the clouds.

4. Lana was happy when she _____ some of her friends at the mall.

5. Mr. Parker _____ his hand and greets anyone who passes by his house.

6. Marvin's drum teacher thought he had the _____ for being a famous musician.

7. The students were surprised by the _____ of food offered in the cafeteria.

8. Even after closing the door, Howard could hear the

_____ sounds of the television.

Writing

What do you think it would be like to visit the depths of the ocean? Write a paragraph telling your thoughts. Use as many of the vocabulary words from the box as you can.

_____

_____

_____

_____

_____

_____

_____

_____

Zeus

Read the story. Think about the meanings of the words in bold type.

Although he is usually lazy, my dog Zeus loves to participate in dog **competitions**. As a result of a series of strange **coincidences**, the International Canine Show was held in my town this year. Zeus was perfect and performed **flawlessly**. He was very energetic for his events. During the obedience trials, he even retrieved a stick thrown by one of the judges—something he would have **scorned** to do if I had thrown it.

As the judges **assessed** the competing dogs, it seemed clear that Zeus was far and away the best. I gave him my **assurances**, though, that I would love him no matter what. Happily, Zeus won the Top Dog trophy! All the judges personally **commended** me for my dog's performance. Zeus just cocked his head and looked at me **mischievously**. Zeus and I knew that he would return to his lazy ways as soon as we returned home.

Look back at the words in bold type. Use clues in the story to figure out the meaning of each word. Write each word on the line next to its meaning.

_____ **1.** determined the value of

_____ **2.** statements that lend support or confidence

_____ **3.** chance events that seem related

_____ **4.** types of contests

_____ **5.** perfectly

_____ **6.** treated as low or bad

_____ **7.** playfully; in a naughty manner

_____ **8.** spoke with approval

Base Words

Base words are words without any endings or other word parts added to them. Some endings are **s**, **ed**, and **ly**. Sometimes the spelling of the base word changes when an ending is added to it.

EXAMPLES: stable   stables   allow   allowing
                crouch   crouched   success   successfully

Write the base word of each word below. Then, use the base word in a sentence.

1. scorned _____

_____

2. mischievously _____

_____

3. assessed _____

_____

4. assurances _____

_____

5. flawlessly _____

_____

6. coincidences _____

_____

7. competitions _____

_____

8. commended _____

_____

Dictionary Skills

A **noun** (**n.**) is a word that names a person, place, thing, or quality.
EXAMPLE: The **dog** walked on a **leash**.

Look at the base words you wrote above. Write three words that are nouns.

_____

_____

Word Wise

scorned	assurances	commended	mischievously
assessed	flawlessly	competitions	coincidences

Rewrite each sentence. Use one of the words from the box in place of a word or phrase in the sentence. Make any changes necessary.

1. Several chance events made Mrs. Jackson believe that she should keep the stray dog.

_____

_____

2. The principal spoke with approval about our teacher, Mr. Butler.

_____

3. The jeweler determined the value of the ring before deciding to buy it for her personal collection.

_____

4. The coach decided that the gymnastic team should attend three contests in the spring.

_____

_____

5. The students treated badly the idea of the library closing immediately after school.

_____

6. The puppy playfully jumped on the coach and ran around the living room.

_____

7. The mayor gave everyone his statements of confidence that the city would build a new school.

_____

_____

8. Marcus played the piano perfectly during his recital.

_____

Writing

Write your own story about a time that you were in a competition. Use as many of the vocabulary words from the box as you can. Use another sheet of paper.

Name _____ Date _____

Unit 4 Assessment

Darken the letter of the word that means the same, or about the same, as the boldfaced word.

1. consult a teacher
- Ⓐ embarked with
- Ⓑ yell at
- Ⓒ talk with
- Ⓓ agree with

2. the building **residents**
- Ⓐ tenants
- Ⓑ offices
- Ⓒ workers
- Ⓓ duties

3. give **consideration** to
- Ⓐ support
- Ⓑ use
- Ⓒ thought
- Ⓓ school

4. the **function** of the room
- Ⓐ size
- Ⓑ shape
- Ⓒ color
- Ⓓ purpose

5. build a **structure**
- Ⓐ collage
- Ⓑ building
- Ⓒ career
- Ⓓ playground

6. a **massive** house
- Ⓐ large
- Ⓑ small
- Ⓒ colorful
- Ⓓ old

7. an **avid** reader
- Ⓐ eager
- Ⓑ uninterested
- Ⓒ careful
- Ⓓ slow

8. a **legendary** musician
- Ⓐ unknown
- Ⓑ young
- Ⓒ recording
- Ⓓ famous

9. lead **expeditions**
- Ⓐ discussions
- Ⓑ journeys
- Ⓒ meetings
- Ⓓ classes

10. paint a **landscape**
- Ⓐ picture of a person
- Ⓑ many people
- Ⓒ picture of the land
- Ⓓ many pictures

11. a **rugged** climb
- Ⓐ rough
- Ⓑ easy
- Ⓒ level
- Ⓓ slippery

12. a **spontaneous** picnic
- Ⓐ small
- Ⓑ crowded
- Ⓒ rainy
- Ⓓ unplanned

13. look at the **profile**
- Ⓐ back of the head
- Ⓑ side of the head
- Ⓒ on top of the head
- Ⓓ below the head

14. a **monumental** mess
- Ⓐ unnecessary
- Ⓑ helpless
- Ⓒ massive
- Ⓓ sticky

Unit 4 Assessment, page 2

Darken the letter of the word that means the same, or about the same, as the boldfaced word.

15. a **versatile** sweater
Ⓐ having many uses
Ⓑ wool
Ⓒ heavy
Ⓓ colorful

16. a difficult **procedure**
Ⓐ trip
Ⓑ book
Ⓒ puzzle
Ⓓ operation

17. manipulate the pictures
Ⓐ rip
Ⓑ paint
Ⓒ move
Ⓓ hang

18. dispatch a police officer
Ⓐ send
Ⓑ honor
Ⓒ find
Ⓓ call

19. watched the **footage**
Ⓐ play
Ⓑ game
Ⓒ film
Ⓓ action

20. lose your **equilibrium**
Ⓐ money
Ⓑ balance
Ⓒ direction
Ⓓ pet

21. turbulent water
Ⓐ flowing
Ⓑ violent
Ⓒ cloudy
Ⓓ spring

22. plundering treasures
Ⓐ selling
Ⓑ buying
Ⓒ amazing
Ⓓ stealing

23. looking for **relics**
Ⓐ gold things
Ⓑ broken things
Ⓒ new things
Ⓓ old things

24. a **dubious** story
Ⓐ long
Ⓑ ridiculous
Ⓒ questionable
Ⓓ believable

25. an important **mission**
Ⓐ task
Ⓑ friend
Ⓒ vehicle
Ⓓ animal

26. critically hurt
Ⓐ never
Ⓑ seriously
Ⓒ possibly
Ⓓ always

27. rubbed his **temples**
Ⓐ the sides of forehead
Ⓑ behind the kneecaps
Ⓒ bones of the elbows
Ⓓ bottoms of feet

28. efficient use of time
Ⓐ more
Ⓑ needing
Ⓒ not wasted
Ⓓ poor

Architects

Read the story. Think about the meanings of the words in bold type.

When people want to build a house, they **consult** an architect. An architect designs and draws plans showing what a house will look like when it is complete. However, before an architect can design a house, he or she must consider the **residents** who will live in it. They take into **consideration** the habits and needs of the people. Architects ask many questions and listen carefully to the answers to see what kind of **structure** will suit the people.

Then, the architect plans the building, keeping in mind the **function** of each room. What will the people do inside? Which areas are for work or play? How much **storage** is needed for personal belongings? They even suggest building materials, which might **consist** of limestone, wood, stones, bricks, or stucco. Technological advances make architects very **efficient**. Designs are put on computer and can be quickly and effortlessly altered if the clients change their minds.

Look back at the words in bold type. Use clues in the story to figure out the meaning of each word. Write each word on the line next to its meaning.

_____ **1.** purpose; use

_____ **2.** producing results with the least effort or waste

_____ **3.** include; be made up of

_____ **4.** people who live in a certain place

_____ **5.** a place for storing things

_____ **6.** to go to for advice or information

_____ **7.** something thought about before making a decision

_____ **8.** anything that is built

Name _____ Date _____

Word Groups

Words can be grouped by how they are alike.
EXAMPLE: types of tools: hammer, saw, wrench, screwdriver

Read each group of words. Think about how they are alike. Write the word from the box that best completes each group.

consist	storage	residents	structure
consult	function	efficient	consideration

1. use, purpose, duty, _____

2. advise, discuss, conference, _____

3. pondering, reflection, meditation, _____

4. practical, effective, workable, _____

5. container, chest, cabinet, _____

6. dwellers, inhabitants, tenants, _____

7. building, house, office, _____

8. make up, include, compose, _____

Dictionary Skills

A **verb (v.)** is a word that shows action. However, actions may not show movement. Some verbs are linking verbs and tell what something <u>is</u> or <u>was</u>.
EXAMPLES: Enrico **was** happy.
Enrico **walked** home.

Look at the vocabulary words above. Write the two words that are verbs.

_____

_____

Word Wise

| consist | storage | residents | structure |
| consult | function | efficient | consideration |

Choose the word from the box that makes sense in the sentences below.

1. Mr. Lewis built a shed because he needed more _____ for his tools.

2. Mario went to _____ the teacher before choosing a research topic.

3. The _____ of the kitchen is to prepare and eat food.

4. Kao was so _____ in using his classroom time that he completed his homework before leaving school.

5. Before accepting the job, Mrs. Thompson took into _____ the number of hours she would have to work.

6. The _____ in the apartment building got together to discuss the parking problems.

7. A bridge is a _____ that crosses a body of water.

8. Terry thinks the candy recipe might _____ of sugar, butter, and milk boiled together.

Writing

What kind of house would you like to live in? Write a paragraph describing the perfect house. Use as many of the vocabulary words from the box as you can.

_____

_____

_____

_____

_____

_____

_____

_____

Photojournalism

Read the story. Think about the meanings of the words in bold type.

Jack "Snap" Schott was such an **avid** photographer that he even took pictures on his days off just for fun. Snap was excited to hear the **legendary** explorer Lena Nordstrom would be his next subject. For years, he had read about her groundbreaking Arctic **expeditions**. Nordstrom had spent several winters in the Arctic cataloging temperatures and weather conditions on these long journeys. As a photojournalist, Snap would take many pictures of Nordstrom as she worked. Then, he would choose the photos for a magazine article, using them to tell the story about Nordstrom and her work.

When Snap arrived in the Arctic, he spent the first day taking pictures of the wild **landscape**. He was fascinated with its **rugged** beauty. Then, Snap began to follow Nordstrom as she worked. Since he never planned his shots, he took many **spontaneous** pictures when Nordstrom least expected it. When Snap developed the pictures, he thought the best one showed the **profile** of Nordstrom. She was standing in front of a majestic and **monumental** mountain when he snapped the side view of her head.

Look back at the words in bold type. Use clues in the story to figure out the meaning of each word. Write each word on the line next to its meaning.

_____ **1.** rough and uneven

_____ **2.** the side view of a person's head

_____ **3.** eager

_____ **4.** long journeys made for a reason

_____ **5.** a picture of the land

_____ **6.** famous

_____ **7.** massive; outstanding

_____ **8.** not planned

Antonyms

Antonyms are words with opposite meanings.

EXAMPLES: loud—soft   fast—slow   hard—easy

Match the words in the box with their antonyms listed below. Write the words on the lines.

avid	profile	legendary	monumental
rugged	landscape	expeditions	spontaneous

_____ **1.** smooth

_____ **2.** planned

_____ **3.** unknown

_____ **4.** small

_____ **5.** portrait

_____ **6.** uninterested

_____ **7.** outings

_____ **8.** front view

Dictionary Skills

A dictionary can help you find out how to say, or pronounce, a word. A dictionary has a **pronunciation key** that lists the symbols for each sound. It also gives a familiar word in which the sound is heard. A pronunciation key usually appears on every other page of the dictionary.

a	add	i	it	o͝o	took	oi	oil
ā	ace	ī	ice	o͞o	pool	ou	pout
â	care	o	odd	u	up	ng	ring
ä	palm	ō	open	û	burn	th	thin
e	end	ô	order	yo͞o	fuse	~~th~~	this
ē	equal					zh	vision

ə = { a in *above*   e in *sicken*   i in *possible*
      o in *melon*   u in *circus* }

Example: guitar (gi tar´)

Use the pronunciation key to help you identify the vocabulary words below. Write the regular spelling for each word on the line.

1. (mon yə mənt´ əl) _____

2. (lej´ ən dâr´ ē) _____

3. (av´ id) _____

4. (prō´ fīl) _____

Name _____ Date _____

Word Wise

avid   profile   legendary   monumental
rugged   landscape   expeditions   spontaneous

Use each vocabulary word in the box to write new sentences.

1. _____
2. _____
3. _____
4. _____
5. _____
6. _____
7. _____
8. _____

Writing

If you were a photojournalist, who would you like to take pictures of? Write a paragraph telling about the pictures you would take. Use as many of the vocabulary words from the box as you can.

_____
_____
_____
_____
_____
_____
_____
_____
_____
_____

Computer Graphics

Read the story. Think about the meanings of the words in bold type.

The fact is, computer "paintbox" programs exist right now that can bring almost any image to life. This **versatile** graphics technology has an almost unlimited number of uses. Using computer graphics, a doctor can practice a difficult **procedure** before actually performing the operation. An architect can design a building on screen and **manipulate** the image so that it can be viewed from any direction, even upside down! Filmmakers can **dispatch** their actors to any place in the world—or universe—without ever leaving the studio.

For example, a fictional planet's landscape can be created by computer and then **superimposed** onto the film after the studio **footage** is shot. In the airline industry, computers are often used to **simulate** jet flights, giving pilots a test run while they are safely on the ground. These tests may be so realistic that the pilots actually lose their **equilibrium**. The graphics fool them into feeling off-balance.

Look back at the words in bold type. Use clues in the story to figure out the meaning of each word. Write each word on the line next to its meaning.

_____ **1.** able to perform many tasks

_____ **2.** the steps done in an operation

_____ **3.** move around

_____ **4.** to send

_____ **5.** placed on top of

_____ **6.** film

_____ **7.** imitate; copy

_____ **8.** balance

Name _____ Date _____

Synonyms

A **synonym** is a word that has the same, or almost the same, meaning as another word.
EXAMPLES: small—little   like—enjoy   busy—active

Write the letter of the synonym beside each word.

_____ **1.** equilibrium   **A.** overlaid

_____ **2.** footage   **B.** send

_____ **3.** dispatch   **C.** move

_____ **4.** procedure   **D.** operation

_____ **5.** simulate   **E.** balance

_____ **6.** superimposed   **F.** film

_____ **7.** manipulate   **G.** having many uses

_____ **8.** versatile   **H.** imitate

Dictionary Skills

 A **syllable** is a part of a word that is pronounced at one time. Dictionary entry words are divided into syllables to show how they can be divided at the end of a writing line. A hyphen (-) is placed between syllables to separate them.
EXAMPLE: computer   com-pu-ter

Find each word in a dictionary. Then, write each word with a hyphen between each syllable.

1. dispatch _____

2. footage _____

3. manipulate _____

4. versatile _____

5. superimposed _____

6. equilibrium _____

7. procedure _____

8. simulate _____

Word Wise

dispatch	simulate	procedure	superimposed
footage	versatile	manipulate	equilibrium

Choose the word from the box that makes sense in the sentences below.

1. Tightrope walkers must have good _____ to keep them from falling.

2. The newspaper had to _____ a person to report on the fire.

3. Our teacher showed us _____ of a volcano erupting.

4. Dr. Moreno said the _____ to remove the stitches could be done in his office.

5. Meg planned to do a science experiment that would _____ an ocean wave.

6. For his party invitation, Max _____ a picture of himself on top of Mount Rushmore.

7. Bonnie bought a _____ shirt that could be worn with jeans or a skirt.

8. Mr. Todd had to _____ the photos so they would all fit on the page.

Writing

Write a paragraph telling how you use a computer. Use as many of the vocabulary words from the box as you can.

_____

_____

_____

_____

_____

_____

_____

_____

_____

Rescue Pilot

Read the story. Think about the meanings of the words in bold type.

The search helicopter bumped through the **turbulent** wind of the storm. Chan hoped the wind would stop soon. She was on a **mission** to find a plane that had gone down several hours before. Her radio had picked up the faint **transmission** from the downed plane, but nothing else had been heard since. Chan hoped to **glimpse** something that would **indicate** the plane's location. She rubbed the **temples** of her forehead where they were beginning to throb. Chan was worried because she didn't have much fuel left.

"Where could they be?" Chan asked herself.

All of a sudden, the radio popped and cracked. Then, Chan heard **frantic** voices. The people had seen her helicopter. With a sigh of relief, Chan was able to talk with one of the passengers and determine their location. While the people were shaken and bruised, no one was **critically** injured. She would be able to rescue them shortly.

Look back at the words in bold type. Use clues in the story to figure out the meaning of each word. Write each word on the line next to its meaning.

_____ **1.** the passage of radio waves through space

_____ **2.** violent

_____ **3.** seriously

_____ **4.** show; point out

_____ **5.** a brief view

_____ **6.** the sides of the forehead

_____ **7.** a special job or task

_____ **8.** very excited with worry or fear

Multiple Meanings

Some words have more than one meaning. You can use clues in the sentence to tell which meaning the word has.

EXAMPLE: subjects

meaning A: courses of study in school. Of all the **subjects**, science is my favorite.

meaning B: people under the control of a ruler. The king greets his **subjects**.

Write the letter of the correct meaning next to each sentence.

transmission

meaning A: the passage of radio waves through space

meaning B: the gears in a car that help the wheels turn

_____ **1.** The mechanic had to repair the car's transmission.

_____ **2.** The radio transmission was not very clear.

temples

meaning A: the sides of the forehead

meaning B: buildings for worship

_____ **3.** Some of the old temples in India had been built of the finest marble.

_____ **4.** When the ball hit Jarred on one of his temples, his mother took him to the doctor.

mission

meaning A: a special job or task

meaning B: a place where a group of religious people promote good will

_____ **5.** The divers were on a mission to recover the sunken ship.

_____ **6.** The Spanish priests that lived in the mission started a school to teach the Native Americans how to read.

Word Wise

temples	glimpse	critically	transmission
mission	indicate	turbulent	frantic

Choose the word from the box that makes sense in the sentences below.

1. When Melvin dyed his hair green, the _____ of his forehead were dyed, too.

2. The map did not _____ where the next rest area could be found.

3. The river was closed to rafting because of _____ water.

4. The park rangers were on a _____ to find the lost child.

5. Joan caught a _____ of the robber before he jumped into the car.

6. The radio _____ between the pilot and control tower was filled with static.

7. Mrs. Andrews raced to her child when she heard the _____ cry for help.

8. The ambulance arrived to take the _____ injured man to the hospital.

Writing

Write your own story about a time you searched for something. Use as many of the vocabulary words from the box as you can.

_____

_____

_____

_____

_____

_____

_____

_____

_____

_____

Archeologist

Read the story. Think about the meanings of the words in bold type.

After months of careful **excavation**, the famous archeologist Dr. Idaho Smith had dug through the final layer of rock. He stood among large piles of **debris** that were left from his efforts to uncover the buried tomb. His experienced eye had detected a small **crevice** in the otherwise solid stone wall. It was the outline of a **massive** door that was nearly twenty feet tall. The figures carved on the stone wall seemed to stare **ominously**, and their angry expressions made him shiver. Still, he knew his real enemy was a stranger who had visited the site claiming to be a reporter. Dr. Smith thought the claim was **dubious** and suspected that the stranger might consider **plundering** the tomb and selling its treasures for his own profit. After all, **relics** like jewelry and statues were quite valuable.

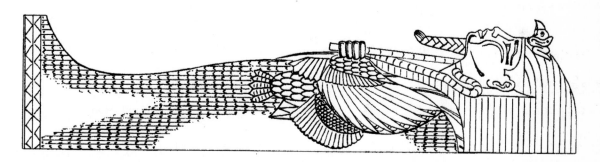

Look back at the words in bold type. Use clues in the story to figure out the meaning of each word. Write each word on the line next to its meaning.

_____ **1.** a narrow opening, caused by a split or crack

_____ **2.** scattered fragments or remains

_____ **3.** questionable; suspect

_____ **4.** a hollowing or carving out

_____ **5.** stealing goods or property

_____ **6.** in a threatening manner

_____ **7.** huge; enormous

_____ **8.** things that survive from the distant past

Name _____   Date _____

Analogies

An **analogy** shows how two words go together in the same way as two other words.
EXAMPLE: Glass is to break as paper is to tear.

Think about how the words in the first pair go together. Write the word from the box to complete the analogy.

debris	crevice	ominously	excavation
relics	dubious	massive	plundering

1. Deep is to cave as narrow is to _____.

2. Books are to libraries as _____ are to museum.

3. Short is to long as tiny is to _____.

4. Doctor is to surgery as archeologist is to _____.

5. Friends are to sharing as thieves are to _____.

6. Hungrily is to starved as _____ is to threatened.

7. Forbidding is to uninviting as _____ is to questionable.

8. Gathered is to firewood as scattered is to _____.

Dictionary Skills

A **noun (n.)** is a word that names a person, place, thing, or quality.
EXAMPLE: The **architect** used a **chisel** to carefully cut away the **rock**.

Look at the vocabulary words in the box above. Write the four words that are nouns.

_____

_____

Word Wise

debris	crevice	ominously	excavation
relics	dubious	massive	plundering

Rewrite each sentence. Use one of the words from the box in place of a word or phrase in the sentence. Make any changes necessary.

1. It took the worker over an hour to cut down the enormous tree.

   _____

2. The archeologist made a carving out in the rock to look for old dinosaur bones.

   _____

3. The fragments and trash from the concert lay scattered in the park.

   _____

4. Long ago, pirates made a living stealing goods from other ships.

   _____

5. While the table looked old, Mara thought that the claim of its being an antique was questionable.

   _____

   _____

6. The lizard ran into a narrow opening in the rock to get away from the bird.

   _____

7. The museum created a display of old Native American baskets, paintings, and other things from the distant past.

   _____

   _____

8. The scary music played threateningly in the haunted house, making the children quake with fright.

   _____

   _____

Writing

What do you think it would be like to open an Egyptian tomb? Write your own story about what you might find. Use as many of the vocabulary words from the box as you can. Use another sheet of paper.

Unit 5 Assessment

Darken the letter of the correct answer.

1. Which of the following prefixes can be added to the root word *violent* to make a new word?
   - Ⓐ non
   - Ⓑ un
   - Ⓒ dis
   - Ⓓ re

2. Which of the following suffixes can be added to the root word *snow* to make a new word?
   - Ⓐ ly
   - Ⓑ ful
   - Ⓒ y
   - Ⓓ less

3. Choose the homophone that correctly completes the sentence.
   Lisa bought _____ CDs.
   - Ⓐ to
   - Ⓑ too
   - Ⓒ two
   - Ⓓ toe

4. Choose the homophone that correctly completes the sentence.
   Abe tripped over a big tree _____.
   - Ⓐ route
   - Ⓑ rude
   - Ⓒ root
   - Ⓓ rule

5. Choose the homophone that correctly completes the sentence.
   Rex took his dog _____ a walk.
   - Ⓐ for
   - Ⓑ four
   - Ⓒ fur
   - Ⓓ fore

6. Which prefix makes *caution* mean "to take caution before"?
   - Ⓐ non
   - Ⓑ pre
   - Ⓒ re
   - Ⓓ un

7. Which prefix makes *behave* mean "not behave"?
   - Ⓐ mis
   - Ⓑ pre
   - Ⓒ in
   - Ⓓ un

8. Choose the word that gives the meaning of the underlined prefix.
   Jan had to <u>re</u>pay money to a friend.
   - Ⓐ not
   - Ⓑ always
   - Ⓒ again
   - Ⓓ with

9. Choose the root word of *readable*.
   - Ⓐ ble
   - Ⓑ mis
   - Ⓒ re
   - Ⓓ read

10. Choose the root word of *joyfully*.
    - Ⓐ full
    - Ⓑ ly
    - Ⓒ oy
    - Ⓓ joy

11. Choose the prefix that means "opposite of."
    - Ⓐ less
    - Ⓑ ly
    - Ⓒ un
    - Ⓓ ible

Unit 5 Assessment, page 2

Darken the letter of the correct answer.

12. Which word comes from the Latin root *cent*, which means "hundred"?
    - (A) accent
    - (B) descent
    - (C) central
    - (D) century

13. Which sentence does the homophone *mane* correctly complete?
    - (A) We live in the state of _____.
    - (B) Tina brushed the _____ of the horse.
    - (C) The _____ idea of soccer is to score goals.
    - (D) We live on the _____ street in town.

14. Choose the sentence in which the word *road* or *rode* is used incorrectly.
    - (A) This road is very bumpy.
    - (B) Roger road his bike down the path.
    - (C) Who rode my bike?
    - (D) Eric rode a gentle horse.

15. Which of the following suffixes can be added to the root word *end* to make a new word?
    - (A) ly
    - (B) able
    - (C) ish
    - (D) less

16. Which suffix changes the word *sing* to mean "one who sings"?
    - (A) ful
    - (B) er
    - (C) ed
    - (D) or

17. Which word comes from the Spanish word *mosca*?
    - (A) mosquito
    - (B) friend
    - (C) alligator
    - (D) brick

18. Which suffix should be added to the word *self* to form a word that means "relating to the self"?
    - (A) or
    - (B) ly
    - (C) al
    - (D) ish

19. Which is the root word of *beautiful*?
    - (A) beau
    - (B) ty
    - (C) beauty
    - (D) ful

20. Choose the pair of homophones that correctly completes the sentence.
    John's _____ shoes rub his _____.
    - (A) knew/heal
    - (B) new/heel
    - (C) gnu/heal
    - (D) new/he'll

21. Choose the pair of homophones that correctly completes the sentence.
    Jill wants _____ eat a _____ for lunch.
    - (A) to/pare
    - (B) too/pair
    - (C) to/pear
    - (D) two/pair

22. Choose the prefix that can be added to the root word *usual* to form a new word.
    - (A) re
    - (B) pre
    - (C) ill
    - (D) un

23. Which Latin prefix means "water"?
    - (A) aqu
    - (B) man
    - (C) chronos
    - (D) tele

Name _____ Date _____

Prefixes

A **prefix** is a syllable added to the beginning of a word to change the meaning of the word. Some prefixes have one meaning, and others have more than one meaning.

EXAMPLES: The baby is dependent. The adult is <u>in</u>dependent. (prefix = in; base word = dependent)

Prefix	Meaning
dis, in, non	not, lack of, the opposite of
im, un	not
mis	bad(ly), wrong(ly)
pre	before
re	again, back

Complete each sentence by adding a prefix from the box above to the word in ( ).

1. (practical) It is _____ to put a new monkey into a cage with other monkeys.

2. (behave) The monkeys might _____ with a newcomer among them.

3. (easy) They will also feel quite _____ for a number of days or even weeks.

4. (violent) Even if the new monkey is _____ in nature, the others may harm it.

5. (usual) Sometimes animal behavior can be quite _____.

6. (cautions) Animal workers take many _____ to keep a new monkey safe.

7. (plan) They carefully _____ how to help the new monkey adjust in its new home.

8. (arrange) They might even _____ the environment to help the newcomer.

9. (patient) The workers cannot be _____ or move too quickly.

10. (appointed) Usually, the workers will not be _____ , and the new monkey will become accepted.

More Prefixes

Remember that a **prefix** is a syllable added to the beginning of a word to change the meaning of the word. The part of the word that the prefix is added to is called a **base** word or **root** word. Some prefixes have one meaning, and others have more than one meaning.

EXAMPLE: Julio is happy. Julio is **un**happy. (prefix = un; base word = happy)

Prefix	Meaning	Example
dis	away, off, lack of, not	disappear
extra	outside of, beyond	extraordinary
fore	before in time or place	forecast
il	not	illegal
im	not	impossible
in	not	inactive
mis	incorrectly	misuse
over	too much	overdo
pre	before	preview
re	again, back	repay
un	opposite of, not	untrue

Complete each sentence using a word that has the same meaning as the words in ( ). Each word should begin with a prefix from the list above.

1. Many people have accomplished (beyond the ordinary) _____ things.

2. Harriet Tubman brought more than 300 slaves out of the South, and she never (led badly) _____ one of them.

3. Louis Pasteur would not (not continue) _____ his work until he had overcome rabies.

4. Robert Goddard was considered (too confident) _____ until he proved that rockets could fly with liquid fuel.

5. Elizabeth Kenny showed great (sight ahead) _____ in her plans for helping polio victims to (gain back) _____ their strength.

Prefixes in Context

Choose the word from the box that makes sense in the sentences below.

disturbing	immediate	uneasy	protection	communicate
uncertain	unpleasant	incredible	impossible	precautions

MEMO

To: Commander Young
From: Carl Digger

   This may be the last time I can **(1)** _____ with you,

as Giles and I are in **(2)** _____ danger. We have been

working daily to excavate the new site. But yesterday we encountered a

(3) _____ situation that has left us feeling

(4) _____. Two **(5)** _____

characters made it clear that we should stop our work. We are

(6) _____ of the reason for the threat. We think they

work for a man who wants the land to build a shopping center. But it is

(7) _____ to stop now! Giles and I have found some

(8) _____ relics and ancient writings. We are taking

many **(9)** _____ at the excavation site, and we have

hired a guard for **(10)** _____.

Writing

Write a response to Carl Digger as if you are Commander Young. Use as many words with prefixes as you can.

_____

_____

_____

_____

Name _____ Date _____

Suffixes

A **suffix** is a syllable added to the end of a word to change the meaning of the word.
EXAMPLES: The explorers have no fear. The explorers are fear<u>less</u>.

Suffix	Meaning
able	is, can be
al	relating to, like
ful	full of
less	without, not able to do
ous	full of
y	having, full of

Add a suffix from the list above to the base word in ( ). Write the new word.

1. Switzerland is a _____

country. (mountain)

2. The Swiss people have a great deal of

_____ pride. (nation)

3. Many Swiss are _____

about several languages. (knowledge)

4. There are an _____

number of activities to do in Switzerland. (end)

5. Many tourists visit the country's

_____ slopes to ski each year. (snow)

6. People who ski know they should be _____ on the steep slopes. (care)

7. Some tourists come to hike on the _____ trails. (beauty)

8. If you hike, it is _____ to have a walking stick. (help)

9. Some people just visit the _____ towns. (remark)

10. However, most tourists are _____ when they leave this wonderful

country. (sorrow)

Name _____   Date _____

More Suffixes

Remember that a **suffix** is a syllable added to the end of a word to change the meaning of the word or the way the word is used. The part of the word that the suffix is added to is called a **base** word or **root** word.

EXAMPLE: The child is quiet. The child played quiet**ly**.

(base word = quiet; suffix = ly)

Noun-forming Suffixes

er	one who	sing<u>er</u>
or	one who	direct<u>or</u>
ness	state or quality of	gentle<u>ness</u>
ment	action or process	appoint<u>ment</u>

Verb-forming Suffixes

en	to make	bright<u>en</u>
ate	to make	liber<u>ate</u>

Adjective-forming Suffixes

able	able to be	laugh<u>able</u>
ern	direction	west<u>ern</u>
ful	full of	care<u>ful</u>
ish	relating to	self<u>ish</u>
less	without	care<u>less</u>
y	state or quality of	storm<u>y</u>

Adverb-forming Suffixes

ly	in a certain way	slow<u>ly</u>
ways	in the manner of	side<u>ways</u>

Add the kind of suffix given in ( ) to each word. Then, on the back of this paper or on a separate sheet of paper, write a sentence with each word you have formed. You may have to change the spelling.

1. sail _____
(noun)

2. fear _____
(adjective)

3. all _____
(adverb)

4. active _____
(verb)

5. kind _____
(noun)

6. might _____
(adjective)

7. conquer _____
(noun)

8. happy _____
(noun)

9. light _____
(verb)

10. cloud _____
(adjective)

11. sudden _____
(adverb)

12. quiet _____
(adverb)

13. fast _____
(verb)

14. play _____
(noun, adjective)

15. wonder _____
(adjective)

16. teach _____
(noun)

Suffixes in Context

Choose the word from the box that makes sense in the sentences below.

eastern	instructor	development	brighten	joyful	thoughtful
painter	fortunate	considerable	swiftly	careful	

Ricardo was an **(1)** _____ who taught painting classes at a small art store.

Ricardo hoped to be a famous **(2)** _____ some day. He lived in an apartment on

the **(3)** _____ side of the building. Ricardo chose this apartment because the

morning sun would **(4)** _____ his art studio so he could see the natural colors of

the pictures he painted. He was **(5)** _____ that he did not have to be at work

until noon. This gave Ricardo **(6)** _____ time to work on his paintings.

Sometimes, Ricardo was quite **(7)** _____ about how a picture should look. He

was very **(8)** _____ to include the smallest details in the painting. At other

times, Ricardo painted **(9)** _____ and would complete a picture in less than a

day. One day, Ricardo got a call from a local art gallery. They wanted to display some of his

paintings. Ricardo was very **(10)** _____ over this new

(11) _____ in his plans to become a famous painter.

Writing

Write your own story about a goal you worked toward. Use as many words with suffixes as you can.

_____

_____

_____

_____

_____

_____

_____

Name _____ Date _____

Latin Roots

Many English words come from the same Latin root.

EXAMPLE: The Latin root *cap* means "head."

English words with the Latin root *cap*: cap, captain, capitol

Latin Root	Meaning
aqu	water
cent	hundred
man	hand

Choose the word from the box that matches the meaning. Use the chart above to help you.

aquarium	aquifer	aquamarine	centipede	century
centimeter	manual	manuscript	manage	

1. a metric unit of measurement _____

2. to handle with skill _____

3. a glass tank for animals that live in water _____

4. an insect with many legs _____

5. worked or done by hand _____

6. a document that is written by hand or typed _____

7. a period of one hundred years _____

8. a pale blue to light green color _____

9. an area of rock that holds water _____

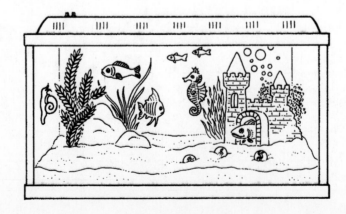

Name _____ Date _____

Greek and Latin Roots

Many words in English come from Greek and Latin roots.

EXAMPLE: biography – a written history of a person's life

from the Greek words *bios* meaning "life" and *graphein* meaning "to write"

GREEK ROOTS	
Word	**Meaning**
metron	measure
bios	life
graphein	to write
tele	far away
hydra	water
skopein	look at
chronos	time

LATIN ROOTS	
Word	**Meaning**
spec	look or see
dict	say
mot	move

Choose the word from the box that matches the meaning.

remote	telegraph	telescope	spectacular
chronometer	hydroscope	biography	dictionary

1. This allows you to write to people far away. _____

2. This is a true story of someone's life written by another person. _____

3. This means "great to look at." _____

4. This allows you to look at something under water. _____

5. This is a book about the words we say. _____

6. This allows you to measure time very accurately. _____

7. This allows you to look at something far away. _____

8. This word means "moved far away from." _____

Name _____ Date _____

Prefixes, Suffixes, and Root Words

Many English words are made of a combination of prefixes, suffixes, and root words. Knowing the meanings of the different parts of a word can help you find the meaning of the word.

EXAMPLE: reactor   =   one who does something again

prefix **re**   =   again

root **act**   =   to do

suffix **or**   =   one who

Root	Meaning
vend	to sell
ver	to turn
var	different
port	to carry
spec	to see
tort	to twist

Prefix	Meaning
con	with
trans	across, beyond, over

Suffix	Meaning
able	able to be
ious	full of
or	one who

Use the meanings in the chart to answer the questions below.

1. What do you think spectacles are used for?

_____

2. What is an ice cream vendor?

_____

3. Name various colors.

_____

4. Name something portable.

_____

5. Draw a picture of a contorted face.

6. Draw lines that converge.

Name _____ Date _____

Homophones

Homophones are words that sound the same but have different meanings and usually different spellings.

EXAMPLES: root, route

Root means "a part of a plant that grows into the earth." A carrot is really a **root**.

Route means "a road taken in traveling." We looked at a map to find the shortest **route**.

Use the sets of homophones below to complete the sentence.

1. to   two   too

The _____ boys wanted Mr. Alton _____

sleep in the tent, _____.

2. he'll   heal   heel

John's _____ will _____ sooner if

_____ just stay off his feet.

3. ere   air   heir

Prince Chang wanted to reward Tang for the merry _____ he fiddled,

and _____ Chang could stop himself, he let slip that he was

_____ to the throne.

4. gnu   knew   new

Lena _____ that a _____ likes to eat the

_____ growth of plants.

5. for   fore   four

The _____ men stood at the _____ of the ship

_____ almost an hour.

6. pear   pare   pair

The _____ of girls wanted to _____ the

_____ before eating it.

More Homophones

Remember that **homophones** are words that sound the same but have different meanings and usually different spellings.

EXAMPLES: to, two, too   write, right   hear, here

Read each pair of words in ( ). Then, complete each sentence by writing the word from the pair that makes sense.

1. (road, rode) The trail that we _____ down this morning took us straight

to the _____ that leads up a mountain.

2. (bare, bear) I was glad the horse was willing to _____ me across the

_____, dry mountains.

3. (mane, main) The _____ thing we had to remember was to hold on to

the horse's _____ when we went up the steep trail.

4. (weight, wait) The _____ of all the camping gear slowed one horse

down, so we had to _____ for it to catch up.

5. (rein, rain) I had to _____ in my horse quickly to get it to stop because

some _____ was beginning to fall.

6. (sight, site) The camping _____ we stopped at for the night was a

_____ to behold.

7. (weather, whether) _____ or not we continue on our journey up the

mountain depends on the _____ tomorrow.

Name _____ Date _____

Reading and Writing Homophones

Remember that **homophones** are words that sound the same but have different meanings and usually different spellings.
EXAMPLE:
Band means "a group that plays music."
Banned means "forbidden."
The recordings of that **band** have been **banned** in some countries.

Read each sentence below. Find the homophones that are used incorrectly and underline them. Then, rewrite the sentences using the correct words.

1. No won is aloud to talk during a fire drill.

_____

2. Do you no how to go to the library?

_____

3. When I am board, I right poems.

_____

4. Meesha red a knew book of tall tails.

_____

5. I can knot weight for the flours to grow.

_____

6. The night wore a knew suit of armor.

_____

7. Wee are studying sells in hour science class.

_____

8. We looked at the read necklaces in the store window.

_____

Name _____ Date _____

Words from Spanish

Many English words come from other languages. One language is Spanish.
EXAMPLE: rodeo   The most exciting part of the **rodeo** is bullriding.

Write the English word from the box that comes from each Spanish word.

alligator	tornado	potato
lasso	mosquito	cork

1. This word comes from the Spanish *tronada*. _____

2. This word comes from the Spanish *lazo*. _____

3. This word comes from the Spanish *patata*. _____

4. This word comes from the Spanish *mosca*. _____

5. This word comes from the Spanish *lagarto*. _____

6. This word comes from the Spanish *corcho*. _____

Find other words that come from Spanish. Write them on the lines with their English word. Use the English word in a sentence.

_____

_____

_____

_____

_____

_____

_____

Name _____ Date _____

Words from Other Languages

Many words we use in English come from countries and cultures all around the world.
EXAMPLES: *Ki-tsiap* comes from Chinese. It means "brine of fish." The English word is **ketchup**.
Garer comes from French. It means "to park." The English word is **garage**.

caterpillar	**chocolate**	**robot**	**pajamas**	**puppy**
magazine	**corduroy**	**clown**	**shamrock**	**window**

See if you can figure out what English words are based on the following words from other languages. The languages of origin and the words' literal meanings are shown as clues.

1. *xocoatl* (Aztec; bitter water) _____

2. *corde du roi* (French; corded fabric of the king) _____

3. *poupee* (French; doll) _____

4. *seamrog* (Irish; clover) _____

5. *vindauge* (Scandinavian; an "eye" for the wind) _____

6. *pai-jamah* (Persian; leg garment) _____

7. *catta pilosa* (Latin; hairy cat) _____

8. *robotnik* (Czechoslovakian; little worker) _____

9. *klunni* (Icelandic; clumsy fellow) _____

10. *makhazin* (Arabic; storehouse) _____

Name _____   Date _____

Blended Words

Some words in the English language have been formed by blending two words together to form one meaning.

EXAMPLES: **motel** comes from *motor + hotel*   We spent the night in a **motel**.

telethon comes from *television + marathon*   The **telethon** raises money for important programs viewers like to watch.

Choose the word from the box to identify each blended word. Then, use the word in a sentence.

flare	clash	brunch	slosh
daisy	twirl	chortle	glimmer

1. breakfast + lunch _____

_____

2. chuckle + snort _____

_____

3. slop + slush _____

_____

4. twist + whirl _____

_____

5. gleam + shimmer _____

_____

6. flame + glare _____

_____

7. day's + eye _____

_____

8. clap + crash _____

_____

Fun with Context Clues

Read the sentences. Use context clues to decide what the words in dark print would mean if they were real words. Then, explain why your meanings make sense.

1. Roger and his dad decided to plant a **glonock**.

meaning: _____

explanation: _____

2. They got out a **tryglif** to dig the hole.

meaning: _____

explanation: _____

3. Then, Roger's dad put the plant in the hole and pushed the extra **vim** around the trunk.

meaning: _____

explanation: _____

4. Roger brushed the **flizzen** off his hands.

meaning: _____

explanation: _____

5. Finally, Roger gave the plant some **molota** with a hose.

meaning: _____

explanation: _____

Name _____ Date _____

Fun with Homophone Riddles

Homophones are words that sound the same but have different meanings and usually different spellings.
EXAMPLE: knight and night

Answer each riddle with a pair of homophones. Write your answers with the correct spelling for each word. The first one is done for you.

1. Question: What do you call an adult-sized moan?

Answer: _grown groan_____

2. Question: What do you call a rose made of wheat?

Answer: _____

3. Question: What do you call time that belongs to us?

Answer: _____

4. Question: What do you call an animal with a sore throat?

Answer: _____

5. Question: What do you call a vender of space under a building?

Answer: _____

6. Question: How do you stop animal feet?

Answer: _____

Vocabulary Skills, Grade 6, Answer Key

pages 4–5
1. C, 2. B, 3. C, 4. A, 5. D,
6. D, 7. A, 8. D, 9. A,
10. B, 11. C, 12. C, 13. A,
14. C, 15. C, 16. B, 17. D,
18. A, 19. B, 20. C, 21. B,
22. A, 23. A, 24. C

pages 6–7
1. B, 2. C, 3. A, 4. B, 5. D,
6. C, 7. A, 8. D, 9. C,
10. B, 11. C, 12. A, 13. C,
14. C, 15. A, 16. A, 17. D,
18. C, 19. A, 20. B, 21. D,
22. D, 23. D, 24. C

pages 8–9
1. B, 2. A, 3. D, 4. A, 5. C,
6. D, 7. A, 8. B, 9. C,
10. B, 11. D, 12. C, 13. D,
14. A, 15. C, 16. A, 17. D,
18. C, 19. B, 20. A, 21. D,
22. B, 23. A, 24. D

page 10
1. devoted, 2. striving,
3. courtiers, 4. conversed,
5. bonds, 6. mesmerized,
7. appointed, 8. precisely

page 11
Base Words
Sentences will vary.
1. strive, 2. devote, 3. bond,
4. courtier, 5. precise,
6. appoint, 7. mesmerize,
8. converse
Dictionary Skills
Answer order may vary.
striving; devoted; appointed;
mesmerized; conversed

page 12
1. courtiers, 2. bonds,
3. mesmerized,
4. precisely, 5. striving,
6. appointed, 7. devoted,
8. conversed

page 13
1. bestowed, 2. swerved,
3. implored, 4. clamor,
5. feat, 6. stadium,
7. marathon, 8. exhaustion

page 14
Analogies
1. clamor, 2. implored,
3. feat, 4. marathon,
5. stadium, 6. exhaustion,
7. bestowed, 8. swerved
Dictionary Skills
Answer order may vary.
feat; stadium; marathon;
clamor; exhaustion

page 15
Sentences may vary.
1. Sara swerved to avoid
hitting the cat on the
sidewalk.
2. The football fans stood
and cheered as the
players ran into the
stadium.
3. People from around the
world came to run the
marathon.
4. The mayor bestowed a
medal on the police
officer who had saved
the child trapped by a
flooded river.

5. Mrs. Kendall implored
her son to be careful
during the game because
he had just gotten a cast
off his arm.
6. Muriel felt that skiing
down the steep hill was
quite a big feat.
7. Nancy was near
exhaustion after playing
two softball games in a
row.
8. The clamor of the
audience encouraged the
actors to take another
bow.

page 16
1. nomadic, 2. harsh,
3. intervals, 4. embarked,
5. vast, 6. priority,
7. invaders, 8. barrier

page 17
Synonyms
1. C, 2. D, 3. H, 4. E, 5. A,
6. G, 7. B, 8. F
Dictionary Skills
1. intervals, 2. nomadic,
3. vast, 4. priority

page 18
1. embarked, 2. vast,
3. barrier, 4. priority,
5. nomadic, 6. intervals,
7. invaders, 8. harsh

page 19
1. ration, 2. unwavering,
3. occupation,
4. belligerently,
5. exasperated,
6. disdainfully,
7. frustration, 8. league

page 20
Multiple Meanings
1. A, 2. B, 3. B, 4. A, 5. A,
6. B

page 21
1. exasperated,
2. unwavering,
3. disdainfully, 4. ration,
5. occupation, 6. league,
7. belligerently,
8. frustration

page 22
1. adorned, 2. futile,
3. hostile, 4. humility,
5. revived, 6. summon,
7. persuade, 8. significant

page 23
Antonyms
1. futile, 2. adorned,
3. hostile, 4. significant,
5. summon, 6. revived,
7. humility
Dictionary Skills
Answer order may vary.
futile, significant, hostile

page 24
Sentences may vary slightly.
1. Sara's ring was adorned
with diamonds and
pearls.
2. The clue the detective
found was very
significant in helping to
solve the mystery.

3. Brian apologized to his
father with humility
when he found out that
his father had been right
all along.
4. Before I face the crowd
of reporters, I must
summon all my courage.
5. The dog barked in a
hostile manner when the
cat ran into its yard.
6. Once the ship ran
aground and wrecked, it
was futile to save it.
7. The photographer tried
to persuade Susan into
posing for a picture.
8. When Mrs. Kings
fainted in the store, the
manager revived her.

pages 25–26
1. B, 2. D, 3. A, 4. B, 5. C,
6. A, 7. A, 8. C, 9. D,
10. C, 11. A, 12. D, 13. C,
14. B, 15. B, 16. D, 17. C,
18. A, 19. D, 20. A, 21. A,
22. D, 23. A, 24. B, 25. C,
26. B, 27. A, 28. C

page 27
1. classroom,
2. loudspeaker,
3. self-confident,
4. high-spirited,
5. dress rehearsal,
6. breathtaking,
7. background,
8. stage fright

page 28
Compound Words
Answer order may vary.
1. dress rehearsal,
2. self-confident,
3. breathtaking,
4. high-spirited,
5. background,
6. stage fright,
7. classroom,
8. loudspeaker
Dictionary Skills
Answer order may vary.
self-confident;
breathtaking; high-spirited

page 29
Sentences may vary.
1. Lana thought the view
from the mountaintop
was breathtaking.
2. The students walked into
the classroom when they
heard the bell.
3. After winning the award,
Kira was more self-
confident.
4. Each morning, the
principal makes the
announcements on the
loudspeaker.
5. Mrs. Jenkins thought her
students were too high-
spirited, so she took
them to the gym to play
basketball.
6. The musician got stage
fright and did not want
to play.

7. Fred found that he
needed a chair on stage
when the people did a
dress rehearsal.
8. Keesha is part of the
stage crew that paints
the background.

page 30
1. implication,
2. abominable, 3. reverting,
4. magnitude, 5. disarm,
6. animosity,
7. despondently,
8. condescendingly

page 31
Crossword Puzzle
Across
1. disarm,
6. condescendingly,
8. animosity
Down
2. reverting,
3. abominable,
4. magnitude,
5. despondently,
7. implication

page 32
1. condescendingly,
2. disarm, 3. implication,
4. reverting,
5. despondently,
6. magnitude,
7. abominable, 8. animosity

page 33
1. elective,
2. determination,
3. recommend,
4. assignment,
5. perplexed,
6. procrastinated,
7. conviction,
8. options

page 34
Synonyms
1. conviction, 2. perplexed,
3. elective,
4. procrastinated,
5. options, 6. recommend,
7. assignment,
8. determination
Dictionary Skills
Answer order may vary.
procrastinated; perplexed;
recommend

page 35
1. recommend, 2. options,
3. elective, 4. assignment,
5. determination,
6. conviction,
7. procrastinated,
8. perplexed

page 36
1. mispronounced,
2. casually, 3. flusters,
4. complex, 5. bizarre,
6. sophisticated, 7. recalls,
8. sarcastically

page 37
Antonyms
1. complex,
2. sophisticated,
3. mispronounced,
4. bizarre, 5. recalls,
6. sarcastically, 7. casually,
8. flusters

Dictionary Skills
Answer order may vary.
casually; sarcastically

page 38
1. mispronounced,
2. sophisticated,
3. complex, 4. sarcastically,
5. recalls, 6. flusters,
7. casually, 8. bizarre

page 39
1. applauded,
2. emphasized, 3. aspect,
4. informal, 5. ethnic,
6. dominated, 7. panel,
8. aristocrat

page 40
Word Web
Nouns: panel, aspect,
aristocrat
Verbs: dominated,
emphasized, applauded
Adjectives: informal,
ethnic
Dictionary Skills
1. C, 2. C

page 41
1. aspect, 2. applauded,
3. informal, 4. aristocrat,
5. panel, 6. dominated,
7. ethnic, 8. emphasized

pages 42–43
1. C, 2. D, 3. A, 4. A, 5. B,
6. C, 7. A, 8. D, 9. B,
10. B, 11. A, 12. C, 13. C,
14. D, 15. A, 16. A, 17. D,
18. C, 19. A, 20. D, 21. A,
22. C, 23. B, 24. A

page 44
1. whimpered,
2. discarded, 3. kennels,
4. snuggled,
5. caressed,
6. enthusiastically,
7. boisterously,
8. antics

page 45
Base Words
1. kennel, 2. snuggle,
3. boisterous, 4. antic,
5. discard, 6. whimper,
7. enthusiastic, 8. caress
Dictionary Skills
Answers order may vary.
boisterously;
enthusiastically

page 46
Sentences may vary.
1. The baby snuggled in its
mother's arms.
2. Leo discarded the empty
milk carton.
3. The students shouted
enthusiastically (or
boisterously) on the last
day of school.
4. Cindy has a job after
school feeding the
animals at some kennels.
5. Mrs. Quan laughed at
the antics of her cat as it
chased a ball of yarn.
6. The baby whimpered
before it went to sleep.

page 46 cont'd
7. Erin watched the monkeys climb boisterously around their cage.
8. Tia's cat always purred when she caressed it.

page 47
1. aggressive, 2. remote, 3. bulky, 4. distinctive, 5. mend, 6. intimidating, 7. retrieve, 8. haughty

page 48
Synonyms and Antonyms
1. synonyms, 2. antonyms, 3. antonyms, 4. antonyms, 5. synonyms, 6. antonyms, 7. antonyms, 8. synonyms
Dictionary Skills
Answer order may vary.
intimidating, bulky, remote, haughty, distinctive, aggressive

page 49
1. haughty, 2. retrieve, 3. mend, 4. remote, 5. distinctive, 6. aggressive, 7. bulky, 8. intimidating

page 50
1. carnivorous, 2. binoculars, 3. migration, 4. hibernation, 5. prey, 6. caribou, 7. predator, 8. tundra

page 51
1. binoculars, 2. carnivorous, 3. prey, 4. migration, 5. hibernation, 6. predator, 7. tundra
Answer: caribou

page 52
Sentences will vary.

page 53
1. submersible, 2. potential, 3. diversity, 4. waves, 5. minute, 6. faint, 7. encountered, 8. luminous

page 54
1. B, 2. A, 3. A, 4. B, 5. B, 6. A

page 55
1. submersible, 2. minute, 3. luminous, 4. encountered, 5. waves, 6. potential, 7. diversity, 8. faint

page 56
1. assessed, 2. assurances, 3. coincidences, 4. competitions, 5. flawlessly, 6. scorned, 7. mischievously, 8. commended

page 57
Base Words
Sentences will vary.
1. scorn, 2. mischievous, 3. assess, 4. assurance, 5. flawless, 6. coincidence, 7. competition, 8. commend
Dictionary Skills
Answer order may vary.
assurance; coincidence; competition

page 58
Sentences may vary.
1. Several coincidences made Mrs. Jackson believe that she should keep the stray dog.
2. The principal commended our teacher, Mr. Butler.
3. The jeweler assessed the ring before deciding to buy it for her personal collection.
4. The coach decided that the gymnastic team should attend three competitions in the spring.
5. The students scorned the idea of the library closing immediately after school.
6. The puppy mischievously jumped on the coach and ran around the living room.
7. The mayor gave everyone his assurances that the city would build a new school.
8. Marcus played the piano flawlessly during his recital.

pages 59–60
1. C, 2. A, 3. C, 4. D, 5. B, 6. A, 7. A, 8. D, 9. B, 10. C, 11. A, 12. D, 13. B, 14. C, 15. A, 16. D, 17. C, 18. A, 19. C, 20. B, 21. B, 22. D, 23. D, 24. C, 25. A, 26. B, 27. A, 28. C

page 61
1. function, 2. efficient, 3. consist, 4. residents, 5. storage, 6. consult, 7. consideration, 8. structure

page 62
Word Groups
1. function, 2. consult, 3. consideration, 4. efficient, 5. storage, 6. residents, 7. structure, 8. consist
Dictionary Skills
Answer order may vary.
consist; consult

page 63
1. storage, 2. consult, 3. function, 4. efficient, 5. consideration, 6. residents, 7. structure, 8. consist

page 64
1. rugged, 2. profile, 3. avid, 4. expeditions, 5. landscape, 6. legendary, 7. monumental, 8. spontaneous

page 65
Antonyms
1. rugged, 2. spontaneous, 3. legendary, 4. monumental, 5. landscape, 6. avid, 7. expeditions, 8. profile
Dictionary Skills
1. monumental, 2. legendary, 3. avid, 4. profile

page 66
Sentences will vary.

page 67
1. versatile, 2. procedure, 3. manipulate, 4. dispatch, 5. superimposed, 6. footage, 7. simulate, 8. equilibrium

page 68
Synonyms
1. E, 2. F, 3. B, 4. D, 5. H, 6. A, 7. C, 8. G
Dictionary Skills
Answers may vary depending on the dictionary used.
1. dis-patch, 2. foot-age, 3. ma-nip-u-late, 4. ver-sa-tile, 5. su-per-im-posed, 6. e-qui-lib-ri-um, 7. pro-ce-dure, 8. sim-u-late

page 69
1. equilibrium, 2. dispatch, 3. footage, 4. procedure, 5. simulate, 6. superimposed, 7. versatile, 8. manipulate

page 70
1. transmission, 2. turbulent, 3. critically, 4. indicate, 5. glimpse, 6. temples, 7. mission, 8. frantic

page 71
Multiple Meanings
1. B, 2. A, 3. B, 4. A, 5. A, 6. B

page 72
1. temples, 2. indicate, 3. turbulent, 4. mission, 5. glimpse, 6. transmission, 7. frantic, 8. critically

page 73
1. crevice, 2. debris, 3. dubious, 4. excavation, 5. plundering, 6. ominously, 7. massive, 8. relics

page 74
Analogies
1. crevice, 2. relics, 3. massive, 4. excavation, 5. plundering, 6. ominously, 7. dubious, 8. debris
Dictionary Skills
Answer order may vary.
debris; crevice; excavation; relics

page 75
Answers may vary.
1. It took the worker over an hour to cut down the massive tree.
2. The archeologist made an excavation to look for old dinosaur bones.
3. The debris from the concert lay scattered in the park.
4. Long ago, pirates made a living plundering goods from other ships.
5. While the table looked old, Mara thought that the claim of its being an antique was dubious.
6. The lizard ran into a crevice in the rock to get away from the bird.
7. The museum created a display of old Native American baskets, paintings, and other relics.
8. The scary music played ominously in the haunted house, making the children quake with fright.

page 76–77
1. A, 2. C, 3. C, 4. C, 5. A, 6. B, 7. A, 8. C, 9. D, 10. D, 11. C, 12. D, 13. B, 14. B, 15. D, 16. B, 17. A, 18. D, 19. C, 20. B, 21. C, 22. D, 23. A

page 78
1. impractical, 2. misbehave, 3. uneasy, 4. nonviolent 5. unusual, 6. precautions, 7. preplan, 8. rearrange, 9. impatient, 10. disappointed

page 79
1. extraordinary, 2. misled, 3. discontinue, 4. over-confident, 5. foresight, regain

page 80
1. communicate, 2. immediate, 3. disturbing, 4. uneasy, 5. unpleasant, 6. uncertain, 7. impossible, 8. incredible, 9. precautions, 10. protection

page 81
1. mountainous, 2. national, 3. knowledgeable, 4. endless, 5. snowy, 6. careful, 7. beautiful, 8. helpful, 9. remarkable, 10. sorrowful

page 82
Sentences will vary.
1. sailor, 2. fearless, fearful, 3. always, 4. activate, 5. kindness, 6. mighty, 7. conqueror, 8. happiness, 9. lighten, 10. cloudy, cloudless 11. suddenly, 12. quietly, 13. fasten, 14. player, playful, 15. wonderful, 16. teacher

page 83
1. instructor, 2. painter, 3. eastern, 4. brighten, 5. fortunate, 6. considerable, 7. thoughtful, 8. careful, 9. swiftly, 10. joyful, 11. development

page 84
1. centimeter, 2. manage, 3. aquarium, 4. centipede, 5. manual, 6. manuscript, 7. century, 8. aquamarine, 9. aquifer

page 85
1. telegraph, 2. biography, 3. spectacular, 4. hydroscope, 5. dictionary, 6. chronometer, 7. telescope, 8. remote

page 86
Accept reasonable answers.
1. seeing, 2. one who sells ice cream, 3. Examples will vary., 4. Examples will vary., 5. Drawings should show an angry or frowning face., 6. Drawings should look like an angle.

page 87
1. two; to; too, 2. heel; heal; he'll, 3. air; ere; heir, 4. knew; gnu; new, 5. four; fore; for, 6. pair; pare; pear

page 88
1. rode; road, 2. bear; bare, 3. main; mane, 4. weight; wait, 5. rein; rain, 6. site; sight, 7. Whether; weather

page 89
Check that students have rewritten the sentence using the correctly spelled words. Underlined words:
1. won; aloud, 2. no, 3. board; right, 4. red; knew; tails, 5. knot; weight; flours, 6. night; knew, 7. Wee; sells; hour, 8. read

page 90
1. tornado, 2. lasso, 3. potato, 4. mosquito, 5. alligator, 6. cork

page 91
1. chocolate, 2. corduroy, 3. puppy, 4. shamrock, 5. window, 6. pajamas, 7. caterpillar, 8. robot, 9. clown, 10. magazine

page 92
Sentences will vary.
1. brunch, 2. chortle, 3. slosh, 4. twirl, 5. glimmer, 6. flare, 7. daisy, 8. clash

page 93
Answers will vary.

page 94
1. grown groan, 2. flour flower, 3. our hour, 4. hoarse horse, 5. cellar seller, 6. pause paws